Great Authors of Children's Literature

Other Books in the History Makers Series:

Great Authors of Children's Literature

By Wendy Mass

Lucent Books
P.O. Box 289011, San Diego, CA 92198-9011

To Stu, for loving Narnia as much as I do.

Library of Congress Cataloging-in-Publication Data

Mass, Wendy, 1967–
    Great Authors of Children's Literature / by Wendy Mass.
        p.   cm. — (History makers)
    Includes bibliographical references (p.   ) and index.
    Summary: Profiles the lives and innovative work of the following pop-
ular authors: A. A. Milne, C. S. Lewis, E. B. White, Dr. Seuss, Roald Dahl,
Maurice Sendak, and Judy Blume.
    ISBN 1-56006-589-3 (lib : alk. paper)
    1. Children's literature, American—History and criticism Juvenile lit-
erature.   2. Children's literature, English—History and criticism Juvenile
literature.   3. Authors, American—20th century Biography Juvenile literature. 4. Authors, English—20th century Biography Juvenile literature.
5. Children's literature—Authorship Juvenile literature. [1. Authors,
American. 2. Authors, English. 3. Literature, American—History and criticism. 4. Literature, English—History and criticism. 5. Authorship.]
I. Title. II. Series.
    PS490.M37   2000
    810.9'282—dc21   99-33564
                                                                          CIP

Copyright 2000 by Lucent Books, Inc.
P.O. Box 289011, San Diego, California 92198-9011

Printed in the U.S.A.

CONTENTS

FOREWORD

The literary form most often referred to as "multiple biography" was perfected in the first century A.D. by Plutarch, a perceptive and talented moralist and historian who hailed from the small town of Chaeronea in central Greece. His most famous work, *Parallel Lives*, consists of a long series of biographies of noteworthy ancient Greek and Roman statesmen and military leaders. Frequently, Plutarch compares a famous Greek to a famous Roman, pointing out similarities in personality and achievements. These expertly constructed and very readable tracts provided later historians and others, including playwrights like Shakespeare, with priceless information about prominent ancient personages and also inspired new generations of writers to tackle the multiple biography genre.

The Lucent History Makers series proudly carries on the venerable tradition handed down from Plutarch. Each volume in the series consists of a set of five to eight biographies of important and influential historical figures who were linked together by a common factor. In *Rulers of Ancient Rome*, for example, all the figures were generals, consuls, or emperors of either the Roman Republic or Empire; while the subjects of *Fighters Against American Slavery*, though they lived in different places and times, all shared the same goal, namely the eradication of human servitude. Mindful that politicians and military leaders are not (and never have been) the only people who shape the course of history, the editors of the series have also included representatives from a wide range of endeavors, including scientists, artists, writers, philosophers, religious leaders, and sports figures.

Each book is intended to give a range of figures—some well known, others less known; some who made a great impact on history, others who made only a small impact. For instance, by making Columbus's initial voyage possible, Spain's Queen Isabella I, featured in *Women Leaders of Nations*, helped to open up the New World to exploration and exploitation by the European powers. Unarguably, therefore, she made a major contribution to a series of events that had momentous consequences for the entire world. By contrast, Catherine II, the eighteenth-century Russian queen, and Golda Meir, the modern Israeli prime minister, did not play roles of global impact; however, their policies and actions significantly influenced the historical development of both their own countries and their regional neighbors. Regardless of their relative importance in the greater historical scheme, all of the figures chronicled in the History Makers series made contributions to posterity; and their public achievements, as well as what is known about their private lives, are presented and evaluated in light of the most recent scholarship.

In addition, each volume in the series is documented and substantiated by a wide array of primary and secondary source quotations. The primary source quotes enliven the text by presenting eyewitness views of the times and culture in which each history maker lived; while the secondary source quotes, taken from the works of respected modern scholars, offer expert elaboration and/or critical commentary. Each quote is footnoted, demonstrating to the reader exactly where biographers find their information. The footnotes also provide the reader with the means of conducting additional research. Finally, to further guide and illuminate readers, each volume in the series features photographs, two bibliographies, and a comprehensive index.

The History Makers series provides both students engaged in research and more casual readers with informative, enlightening, and entertaining overviews of individuals from a variety of circumstances, professions, and backgrounds. No doubt all of them, whether loved or hated, benevolent or cruel, constructive or destructive, will remain endlessly fascinating to each new generation seeking to identify the forces that shaped their world.

INTRODUCTION

Authors who write children's books are a special breed. They are the real Pied Pipers, using their imaginations to lead young people through the maze of childhood. Today hundreds of children's books are published each year, from picture books for toddlers to sophisticated novels for young adults. The authors of today know they stand on the shoulders of the giants of yesterday. These innovative men and women bucked the current trends of their day and created their own. They continually shaped the direction of literature for children, and their books now inhabit the collective memories of generations of readers.

With Winnie-the-Pooh, A. A. Milne perfectly rendered the essence of childhood wonder like no one before or since. Roald Dahl turned childhood into a fantastic adventure in which kids are the ones with power. Dr. Seuss's wild imagination taught young children that reading can be fun, and Maurice Sendak helped them face their fears.

With Narnia, C. S. Lewis swept children into a magical world, and returned them better equipped to find magic in their own lives. In *Charlotte's Web*, E. B. White used his gift as one of America's greatest storytellers to introduce children to life's most important issues—the fight to stay alive, the eventual surrender to death, and the growth and joy that come in between. Contemporary writer Judy Blume let adolescents know they were not alone by realistically portraying young people on the verge of growing up.

These seven authors hailed from both sides of the Atlantic, and they came from very different backgrounds, cultures, and times. Some of them wrote for children all of their lives and produced dozens of books; some only wrote for a few years and produced a handful. Despite all their differences, however, much is the same. All of them loved to read as children and believed they thought differently from everybody else. They all wrote or drew for pleasure from a very young age, and most worked on their high school or college publications. Each recognized the importance of reading in a child's life and was determined to write for

Books capture the essence of childhood wonder, adventure, and imagination.

children and adolescents in a unique way. Although many faced controversy, they all received tremendous praise, financial success, and the adoration of children worldwide. They acknowledged their own good fortune and recognized each other's talents.

Although not technically contemporaries, Seuss, Sendak, White, and Blume were all writing in America in the second half of the twentieth century. This gave them the opportunity to interact with each other. Being both writers *and* artists, Seuss and Sendak ran into each other fairly often. Seuss named Sendak as his favorite children's book creator, with A. A. Milne close behind. Sendak called Seuss "the big Papa" and claimed he was a "mischief-maker and revolutionary who was on the side of the kids."[1] One children's scholar has shown how the books of Seuss and Sendak fit together: "Dr. Seuss's *Cat in the Hat* warned children about upsetting their parents by telling them what really went on 'inside' while the adults were out. But Sendak let the cat out of the bag."[2]

Although she writes very different types of books, Judy Blume has said that as a beginning writer she idolized both Seuss and Sendak. The three of them shared a stage once at the American Bookseller's Convention when they were honored for their work and had been asked to talk about their craft. Today, Blume and Sendak have teamed up to fight censorship in schools and libraries. Blume is also a big fan of E. B. White, and she said recently that *Charlotte's Web* makes her cry every time she reads it and that no child should grow up without it. White and Sendak worked with the same editor, who inspired them both in different ways.

Roald Dahl also wrote his children's books in the later half of the century, but he spent most of his time in England. Nevertheless, he still kept up with the kinds of books being published in America, and after reading *Where the Wild Things Are*, he chose Maurice Sendak as his first choice to illustrate *Charlie and the Chocolate Factory*. Scheduling prevented it, however, and as Dahl's biographer put it, "their never-realized partnership is one of the more tantalizing might-have-beens of children's literature."[3]

A. A. Milne and C. S. Lewis were separated from the others by time and geography. Even though Lewis wrote the Narnia books in the 1950s, he was already near the end of his life. As a young man in the 1920s, however, Lewis did cross paths with Milne, or at least with Milne's work. After returning from a production of Milne's play *The Dover Beach*, Lewis wrote in his journal that it was one of the most amusing things he'd ever seen. The illustrators of Lewis's and Milne's books shared the experience of being linked with those few projects for the rest of their lives. The illustrator of the Narnia books, Pauline Baynes, explains, "I think it's the fate of the illustrator [to be typecast]. Look at Ernest Shepard. He was so brilliant and did so much fine work, but people only associate him with Pooh and Piglet. It's the penalty of hitching your wagon to a star."[4]

As one scholar noted in the *Horn Book Magazine*, the prestigious journal for the study of children's literature, "We desperately need the creators who will give our children books they do not even know they want—until, that is, they read them."[5] The seven authors examined here have done just that. And by doing so, they have become immortalized as the best-selling, most popular children's writers of the twentieth century.

CHAPTER 1

The History and Importance of Writing Books for Children

> Reading as a means of processing information is unique to human experience. I would put reading right up there with the opposable thumb, Michelangelo and milk chocolate in the order of evolutionary milestones.[6]

—E. L. Konigsburg, two-time Newbery Medal winner

Books people read when they are young help define who they grow up to be. They influence their interests, their goals, perhaps even their professions. In the formative years, children's minds are open and ready to soak up information. They need to understand who they are and what it means to be human. Within the small scope of their daily life, their personal experiences are all they have as examples. Children's innate curiosity, however, leads them to want to know more, to hear stories, and eventually to be able to read these stories themselves.

Reading gives children a sense of accomplishment, shows them they can entertain themselves, and sets them on a lifelong path of enjoyment and learning. By observing fictional characters' experiences, children open their minds to new possibilities and learn lessons without realizing they are doing so. They can vicariously live out a life they most likely will never experience, and they can do it from the safe distance of a book. The familiarity of a much-loved book can provide comfort in a way real life often cannot. As C. S. Lewis put it, "We read to seek an enlargement of our being."[7]

The first book written exclusively for children was a book on table manners printed in France around 1487. Because the text was written in rhyme, it became very popular. Children enjoyed the lyrical and rhythmic nature of the language, even though the subject matter was dull. It wasn't until a few centuries later that children would find joy in both the content and the words.

Chapbooks, Mother Goose, and Morality

In the 1600s and 1700s peddlers who traveled from town to town to sell their wares began offering small booklets called "chapbooks." The pages of the little books (which were only a few square inches) were either sewn together or merely folded. Often costing no more than a penny, they were filled with lighthearted accounts of ancient legends, medieval tales, fairy tales, and folktales. Although these chapbooks were looked down upon by adults as silly and wasteful, children adored them and collected them lovingly. It is not surprising that

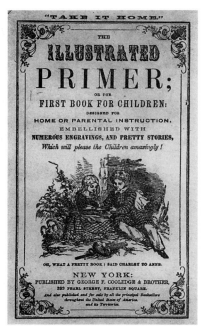

The Illustrated Primer *was the first publication specifically for children in 1691.*

children cherished them so much because their only other reading options were stories written to educate them on morals and manners, often told in morbid, depressing ways.

The pervading belief among educated adults was that books should show children how to live best. The deeply religious Puritans who came to the New World from England filled their children's minds with books like *A Token for Children: An Exact Account of the Conversion, Holy and Exemplary Lives and Joyful Deaths of Several Young Children.* One staple of Puritan education was *The New England Primer,* first published around 1691 with the subtitle *An Easy and Pleasant Guide to the Art of Reading.* Filled with verses like "In Adam's Fall, We Sinned All"; "Thy Life to Mend, This Book Attend"; and "An Idle Fool is Whipt at School," clearly these books were not written with children's enjoyment in mind.

With the publication of Daniel Defoe's 1719 tale of adventure, *Robinson Crusoe,* and Jonathan Swift's 1726 illustrated political satire, *Gulliver's Travels,* children began to read books that were enjoyable. They simply skipped the parts they did not understand, and, eventually, when it became clear that children would be the books' main audience, the more difficult passages were deleted from future editions. It is unclear if *The Tales of Mother Goose,* first published in English in 1729, was intended to be a children's book. This cheerful collection of eight fairy tales was created by a Frenchman named Charles Perrault and included "Sleeping Beauty" and "Cinderella." No matter what the original audience, the name "Mother Goose" became synonymous with nursery rhymes and fairy tales and was seized upon by children everywhere.

The Birth of Fiction

In 1744, English publisher John Newbery published a book called *A Little Pretty Pocket-Book.* This was the first book written solely for the amusement of children. It featured Jack the Giant-killer (the precursor of today's "Jack and the Beanstalk"), who had previously appeared in chapbooks as a more ominous character. This project was so successful that Newbery continued publishing books specifically for children, and in 1765 the first fictional children's novel appeared. It was a big success. *The Renowned History of Little Goody Two Shoes,* attributed to author Oliver Goldsmith, told the story of a poor girl who travels the countryside teaching children to read. More fiction followed, and like the popular nineteenth-century series *Elsie Dinsmore* by Martha Finley, it was always intended to teach a very obvious moral lesson.

The first poetry for children probably would be considered *Original Poems for Infant Minds,* which was published in the 1790s by Ann and Jane Taylor and included "Twinkle, Twinkle, Little Star." A few years later, seeing children's need to expand their literary horizons, Charles Lamb and his sister Mary adapted Shakespeare for children and titled their 1806 collection *Tales from Shakespeare.* This volume is still considered the best of its kind.

Gulliver the giant from Jonathan Swift's novel Gulliver's Travels.

In 1823, the English edition of the Grimm brothers' fairy tales and folktales was published, collecting hundreds of centuries-old stories. The brothers attempted to include all the elements of the original versions, and their collection is the source for most of our modern-day fairy tales. However, these retellings of such famous tales as "Little Red Riding Hood" and "Hansel and Gretel" were not the versions children are familiar with now. The stories were often grim, and typically the characters didn't live happily ever after—no woodsman arrived to rescue Little Red from the wolf in the original version, for example. The Grimm brothers' collection was followed by Hans Christian Andersen's lighter (yet still not cheery) fairy tale adaptations in 1846, and by the time Andrew Lang's popular *Blue Fairy Book* appeared four decades later, publishers knew that books on fairy tales would remain a permanent part of children's literature. Some authorities on children, however, warned parents about letting their children read or even hear fairy tales. Sarah Trimmer, a late eighteenth-century educator, believed fairy tales were immoral "because they taught ambition, violence, a love of wealth, and the desire to marry above one's station."[8]

Whether parents heeded Trimmer's warning, later editions of the tales were often given happier endings, and children's publishing continued to flourish. The popularity of the *Book of Nonsense,* first published in 1846 by respected British artist Edward Lear, proved that if a book is any fun, children *will* want to read it. Filled with humorous verse and illustrations, it was a turning point in the publishing of joyful children's books, and it paved the way for what is considered the first great children's novel.

Through the Rabbit Hole

Lewis Carroll is the pen name for Oxford math professor Charles Lutwidge Dodgson. In 1865, this shy and unassuming man gave the world *Alice's Adventures in Wonderland.* Illustrated with unforgettable drawings by Sir John Tenniel, it is considered to be the first great English novel written for children. There are no moral lessons, just flights of the imagination. Pulitzer prize–winning author Alison Lurie points out in her book *Don't Tell the Grown-ups: Subversive Children's Literature,* "Alice, except for her proper manners, is by no means a good little girl in mid-Victorian terms. She is not gentle, timid, and docile, but active, brave, and impatient. She is highly critical of her surroundings and of the adults she meets."[9] Children were finally able to read about a character like themselves, who wasn't perfect and who dreamed of an escape from her boring surroundings. In America, another respected writer and statesman using a pen name captured more children's hearts. Samuel Clemens, writing as Mark Twain, wrote *The Adventures of Tom Sawyer* as the antithesis to what he called "goody-goody boys' books."[10] His main character lies, steals, swears, and cheats, but children recognized parts of themselves in Tom and his friends. Reading original fiction was finally *fun*.

Around this same time a trio of great illustrators—Walter Crane, Randolph Caldecott, and Kate Greenaway—revolutionized the

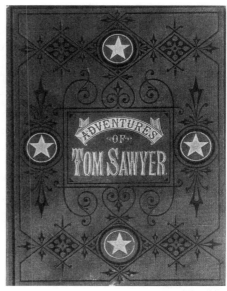

The Adventures of Tom Sawyer *is one of the best-loved children's adventure novels of all time.*

picture-book industry. Since the advent of printing, illustrators had used tools or pencils to etch their work onto wooden blocks or copper plates. These drawings were usually tiny—about the size of a postage stamp—and only exceptional artists could make these drawings come alive. These three artists, with their keen eye for design, were up to the task, and for the first time they could produce their work in color. This process breathed more life into the illustrations, and they began taking up more space on the page. The pictures and the text now complemented each other to make a unified whole. Books like Greenaway's *Under the Window* and Caldecott's *Hey Diddle and Baby Bunting* didn't merely tell good stories; they were works of art and visions of other worlds. They inspired every illustrator who followed.

A Literary Canon Appears

Publishing houses began to respond to the growing number of books for children in the early 1900s. In 1919, Macmillan became the first publishing house to form a separate department to create new children's books. As the number of children's books grew, different genres—adventure stories, mysteries, fantasies—emerged. It is easy to see that the great milestones in each genre paved the way for the classics of the twentieth century. In Britain, fantasy novels were always very popular. Lewis Carroll's nonsensical verse was a precursor to Dr. Seuss's own brand of spirited silliness. George Macdonald's *At the Back of the North Wind* and the novels by Edith Nesbit in which everyday children had magic adventures inspired the work of J. R. R. Tolkien and C. S. Lewis. In the United States, books of "Americana" flourished. A few years before Mark Twain's tales of the South appeared, *Little Women* by Louisa May Alcott was published. A few decades later the *Little House* series by Laura Ingalls Wilder joined the group. These stories are so universal that interest in these titles has never waned. Another favorite genre for old and young was the animal story. Rudyard Kipling's Jungle Books, Beatrix Potter's *The Tale of Peter Rabbit,* and Kenneth Grahame's *The Wind in the Willows* set the stage for *Winnie-the-Pooh* and *Charlotte's Web.*

By the turn of the twentieth century, nearly half of the population in America was under twenty years old. Stricter child labor laws were enforced, and the mandatory years of education increased. These factors contributed to an elongated period of childhood and adolescence. In the first half of the century, one man almost single-handedly delivered thirteen hundred novels written exclusively for children and teenagers.

The Stratemeyer Syndicate and Its Legacy

Edward Stratemeyer grew up reading cheap dime novels and children's magazines. It was his dream to write for children, but he wanted to do it in a new way. The result would revolutionize children's fiction. In a thirty-year span, Stratemeyer created 125 different book series, including *Tom Swift, The Hardy Boys, The Bobbsey Twins, The Rover Boys,* and *Nancy Drew.* If he didn't write the books himself, he wrote the outline and someone else turned it into a book. No matter who actually wrote a particular book, only one name—a fictitious one—would get the credit for each series. For instance, all the Nancy Drew books were published under the name Carolyn Keene, but they were written (and continue to be written) by many different authors (although in the beginning Stratemeyer's daughter Harriet wrote most of them). In 1926, the American Library Association took a poll of the reading preferences of thirty-six thousand children across the country. Much to the librarians' loudly voiced dismay, 98 percent listed titles from Stratemeyer's series as their favorite books. The librarians did not consider the books to be instructive in any way and thought reading them was a waste of time. Today, librarians are the first to admit that any way to get children to read is a good thing.

At the end of the twentieth century, the Nancy Drew books alone have sold more than 90 million copies. No one claims that the Stratemeyer series were great literature, but the timeless stories hooked generations of kids on reading and opened the market for bigger and better books to come.

Bigger and Better

In response to the rising popularity of children's books, a new crop of dedicated, visionary, and mostly female editors appeared on the scene during the 1920s and '30s. By then nearly every major publishing company had a children's book division, and soon publishing houses dedicated *only* to children's books evolved. Editors of these departments strove to entice and nurture only the finest authors and illustrators. They took pride in producing not only wonderful stories but beautifully designed books by authors such as Laura Ingalls Wilder (the *Little House* series), Robert McCloskey *(Make Way for Ducklings)*, and Margaret Wise Brown *(Goodnight Moon)*.

Frederic G. Melcher, the longtime editor of the trade journal *Publisher's Weekly* and champion of children's books and their writers, proposed in 1921 that the American Library Association honor

An illustration by Randolph Caldecott.

great books with a special annual award. In tribute to the great nineteenth-century publisher of children's books John Newbery, the Newbery Medal was created. The highest honor a children's book author can achieve, it is given by the American Library Association each year to celebrate the author who made the most distinguished contribution to American literature for children. And since 1938, in memory of famed illustrator Randolph Caldecott, the Caldecott Medal has been awarded annually to the finest artist/illustrator of an American picture book. Award winners have something special—an innovative plot combined with a unique voice and literary style. These awards raised the standards of children's books, and the quality of the books published continued to improve.

For the next few decades, America's constantly changing society was reflected in the books for its children. The works of British writers continued to be just as popular in America as they were at home, and over the next fifty years, children would be able to choose from an increasing variety of literary material.

Publishing in the Second Half of the Twentieth Century

Nationwide tests conducted in the 1950s caused educators to fear that children were not reading as well as they should be. The response from publishers was a rush of beginning-reader books. Nonfiction books for children written in simple language also started filling library shelves. The number of children's books published annually doubled by the end of the decade.

The turbulent sixties and soul-searching seventies heralded perhaps the greatest changes in books for older children—the birth of realistic fiction that dealt with contemporary social and coming-of-age issues. S. E. Hinton's *The Outsiders* and Judy Blume's *Are You There God? It's Me, Margaret* presented two very different kinds of teen angst and became bestsellers. Gender roles became more flexible as girls and women took on more responsibilities and had more freedom, and the star of Louise Fitzhugh's *Harriet the Spy* became a role model of female independence. As for the younger set, once the preschool and day care movements strengthened, publishers saw the need for simple, playful books for toddlers. Bookstores that sold only children's books grew in number, and now that publishers were finally printing in paperback, children could purchase the books themselves. These independent stores were very successful until they were overshadowed by the chain stores and superstores of the late 1980s and '90s, whose purchasing power and large inventories allow them to sell books at a discount.

By the end of the 1980s, bookstore sales of children's books reached $1 billion. The spirit of Edward Stratemeyer returned in the middle of the decade when series fiction sprang up with a vengeance and proved once again that books do not have to be award-winning literature as long as they're a good read. Ann M. Martin's *Baby-Sitter's Club* and Francine Pascal's *Sweet Valley High* outshone the outdated Nancy Drew series and brought pre-teen girls back to the bookstores.

By the 1990s, horror series like R. L. Stine's *Goosebumps* (which brought preteen *boys* to the bookstores) and tie-ins of popular television shows began to fill the stacks. *Nancy Drew* was reborn, spun off into two new series, and modernized. Series for middle school and younger children have become a way to encourage reluctant younger readers to read for pleasure. And to make sure that they are still reading quality books, award-winning titles for this age group are often incorporated into their curricula at school, as more educators realize how valuable reading fiction is to a young person.

Banning Books

Children's lives today are more complex than in the past. They are under a lot of pressure at school, and the competition to get into college has never been more fierce. Through television, movies, books, and the Internet, they know more about the world than any generation before them. In years past, children were allowed to stay sheltered and naïve quite a bit longer. Some parents and educators today feel they need to protect children from unsafe outside influences and believe that censoring "objectionable" books is one answer. Usually the books that are banned are done so because they deal with mature or potentially frightening subject matter. Popular children's book authors Judy Blume, Maurice Sendak, and Roald Dahl have all spoken out against book banning, which they believe is not in the child's best interest. Progress is slow, and as recently as 1989, two California school districts banned an edition of "Little Red Riding Hood" because one illustration showed Little Red carrying a bottle of wine along with food to her grandmother's house. Two hundred years have passed since parents were warned about the dangers of fairy tales, and still educators are trying to save children from their clutches.

The State of Publishing Children's Literature Today

Today's fast-paced and information-laden society provides a new challenge to children's book writers and publishers. In order to compete with cable television, computer games, and the Internet, publishing children's books has turned from a labor of love into a cutting-edge, competitive business. Fiction, romance, horror, and mystery series continued to be churned out in the late '90s, as do novelty books ("how to" or storybooks packaged with toys or games), biographies of young actors and musicians, and adaptations of popular, youth-oriented television shows and movies. In some ways, the intensive merchandising that goes along with modern-day book publishing keeps the books alive longer. Children's books are now being made into television shows, movies, books-on-tape, and home videos. Stuffed toys and games based on characters from beloved classics can be found in every bookstore and toy store.

Today's children, many of whom don't have the stable home life taken for granted in the past, need great books. They look to books to help fulfill the same needs that children have had throughout history: the need for security, the need to love and be loved, the need to belong, the need to achieve, the need for change, the need for knowledge, the need for beauty and order. Authors writing for children today have a tough assignment. They have to try to fulfill these needs without talking down to their fairly jaded audience, and they have to fulfill them in new, innovative ways, with stories young readers have not heard before. Rising printing costs and strong competition mean publishers need to rely more on their "star" authors whose books they are confident will sell. This makes it more difficult for the new writer to break into the field.

Luckily, there is a wide range of topics available to the writers of the twenty-first century. In the past decade books with a sense of multiculturalism and ethnic diversity have taken a strong hold, expanding children's understanding of other cultures. Since children and teenagers *are* exposed to more of the world than ever before, writers are no longer as limited in their subject matter. Fortunately for children, teachers, and parents, great books continue to be written, to be studied in schools, and to win Newbery and Caldecott awards. Old favorites are constantly reprinted so that no matter where in the world they live, no matter how complicated their life is, every child can experience the special friendship between Christopher Robin and Pooh, can learn how a spider named Charlotte saves the life of a pig, can watch the Cat in the Hat make a mess, can find out if Charlie wins a trip to the Chocolate Factory and if Margaret makes it through puberty, can travel to where the Wild Things are, and discover how Peter, Edmund, Susan, and Lucy find their way through a magic wardrobe into Narnia.

CHAPTER 2

A. A. Milne

As children we have explored [the world of imagination] from end to end, and the map of it lies buried somewhere in our hearts, drawn in symbols whose meaning we have forgotten. A gleam from outside may light it up for us, so that for a moment it becomes clear again, and in that precious moment we can make a copy of it for others.[11]

—A. A. Milne

The most famous children's books to come out of England in the first half of the twentieth century were written by Alan Alexander Milne. As *Life* magazine wrote, "The world of Christopher Robin and Pooh has become so much a part of the world of childhood that children move in it as easily as if Pooh were an everyday friend and his forest a familiar place."[12] Written over a period of five years, Milne's four books for children made such an impact in the world that their presence is still felt as strongly today. In fact, one newspaper recently claimed, "Few people in responsible positions in society today got to eminence without the influence of Pooh."[13]

Milne's stories created a magical, simple world, where a little boy, with the help of his animated stuffed animals, has a whole forest to romp in. Children everywhere embraced the catchy verse, the humor and sentimentality, the beloved characters, and the little boy who brought it all together. The Pooh stories, according to John Rowe Townsend, "are lodged in what could almost be called the folk memories of the twentieth century."[14] The immediate and overwhelming response from readers, literary critics, educators, and the media turned the life of a respected playwright, essayist, and novelist into something quite different, and it turned his son, Christopher Robin, into one of the most famous little boys in the world.

An Ideal Childhood

Alan Alexander Milne was born to Sarah and John Milne on January 18, 1882, in London, England. He had two older brothers, Barry and Ken, and their father ran a school for young boys called Henley House. It was in this environment of learning and camaraderie that the three boys were raised. Milne was very close to his father and his brother Ken, explaining that "there was never any doubt that Barry was mother's darling and that I was father's, leaving poor old Ken to take second place in both their hearts, and first in mine and Barry's."[15]

By any standards, Milne led a wonderful childhood on the cusp of the Victorian and Edwardian eras. He and Ken spent endless hours exploring the streets of London on their bicycles and climbing trees in the nearby countryside. Milne could read by the age of two, and a few years later he convinced his parents to allow him to attend lessons with the other boys at Henley House. One of his teachers was the soon-to-be famous author H. G. Wells, who became a mentor and lifelong friend. When Milne was too old to attend his father's school, he was sent away to study at Westminster School in 1893. At eleven years old, he became the youngest person in the school's history to win a math scholarship, which would one day help him get into college.

Over Christmas vacation in 1899, Milne said he "discovered the itch for writing which has never quite left me"[16] and lost his interest in math. He and Ken wrote lighthearted verse and stories together for the school magazine, and Milne de-

Alan Alexander Milne, creator of the Winnie-the-Pooh series.

cided he wanted to attend Cambridge one day to edit its highly respected humor magazine, *The Granta*. After seven years at Westminster, his plans became a reality. Even though he was attending Cambridge on a math scholarship, Milne spent much of his time in college making a name for himself as a humor writer and, in his last two years, editing the magazine itself. He knew that writing was the career he wanted to pursue, so after graduating in 1903 with a degree in mathematics, he rented an apartment in London and began writing freelance articles for magazines and newspapers. His first article, a parody of Sherlock Holmes, appeared in *Vanity Fair* magazine. He didn't even know it had been accepted until he picked up an issue, casually breezed through it, and thought someone else had stolen his idea. His joy and slight embarrassment at seeing his name in print was a reaction to publication that he would continue to have for the rest of his life.

Early Success

Milne was very single-minded where his writing was concerned. He sent his material to every newspaper and magazine in London, and more often than not, someone published it. After about fourteen months of freelance writing, however, he realized that he was out of money. A book based on his articles called *Lovers in London* was published in 1905 and gave him financial security for a short time. Unfortunately, the book didn't get very good reviews, and a few years later Milne bought back the rights to it so that no one else could republish it. In 1906 he was offered the job of assistant editor at *Punch*, the premier humor magazine of the day. Having published a few pieces with them already, he accepted the position with gratitude and excitement. With typical modesty, he felt "his real achievement . . . was to be not wholly the wrong person in the right spot at the right moment."[17]

As part of his job at the magazine, Milne was required to write an article each week. He found this very stressful. "Ideas may drift into other writers' minds," he lamented, "but they do not drift my way. I have to go and fetch them. I know [nothing] to equal the appalling heartbreaking anguish of fetching an idea from nowhere."[18] Somehow the pieces got written, and Milne was becoming well respected in literary circles. He published a collection of his *Punch* essays called *The Day's Play* and became friends with J. M. Barrie, the author of *Peter Pan*. Milne wanted to expand his horizons so he wrote a short play. Barrie convinced him he had the talent and encouraged him to keep writing. Milne discovered that he enjoyed this type of dramatic writing, and he was fully prepared to devote all his energy to becoming a playwright. What he became instead, however, was a soldier.

Love and War

In 1913, a year before World War I began, Milne married Dorothy (Daphne) de Selincourt, the goddaughter of *Punch*'s editor. He proposed to her in the middle of a snowstorm at a ski resort. The two were well matched in terms of their sense of humor, and they enjoyed each other's company.

In 1914, Milne went off to war. His position as a signal officer kept him away from the action for most of the time. Daphne was also helping with the war effort, and they were allowed to live together near the base. At night Milne dictated stories and plays to Daphne, a collaboration they both enjoyed. He sent a play called *Wurzel-Flummery* to J. M. Barrie, who found some people tentatively interested in producing it. Two days later he was sent to the front lines in France. He fought bravely for a few months, until a severe fever sent him back to his battalion's base in England to recuperate.

Good news awaited him upon his return from France. His play was to be performed along with two one-act plays of Barrie's. Milne was thrilled to share the playbill with his friend and was given leave to see it performed in London. By the time the war was over, Milne's

A. A. Milne and his wife Daphne.

interest in returning to work at *Punch* had waned. Fortunately, the editor didn't seem too excited to have him come back, and he found himself free to put all his efforts into his plays. Now a strong pacifist, he wrote, "It was in 1919 that I found myself once again a civilian. For it makes me almost physically sick to think of that nightmare of mental and moral degradation, the war."[19]

A Playwright and a Child Are Born

Once again back in London, Milne needed a steady job. He took a position as the theater critic for the *Outlook*, but soon realized it was a conflict of interest for a playwright to critique other people's plays. Six weeks later he was out of work again, but fortunately one of his plays would soon hit the stage and he would never have to worry about a day job again. On January 4, 1920, *Mr. Pim Passes By* was performed in London. It was a huge success and became Milne's most popular play.

Now living in a beautiful house on a quiet street in London, Milne quickly became the best-known and highest paid playwright in England. With successful productions like *The Romantic Age* and *The Dover Road* and, later, *The Toad of Toad Hall*, Milne's popularity spread to America. At one point, five of his plays were being performed at the same time, in theaters all across London and New York. As an experiment, he decided to write a mystery novel since there wasn't very much competition in that field at the time. When *The Red House Mystery* was published in 1921, it was highly praised, and it is still considered one of the best of its genre.

On August 21, 1920, Milne was overjoyed to welcome his son, Christopher Robin, into the world. He and Daphne nicknamed the boy Billy, and as soon as he could speak he called himself Billy Moon, since he couldn't pronounce Milne. Milne loved playing with his son and rented a country home on Cotchford Farm (on the edge of Ashdown Forest in Sussex) so that they could be outdoors more. On Christopher Robin's first birthday, he was given a stuffed bear from Harrods department store. The bear was soon joined by a donkey, a small pig, and a kangaroo with a baby in its pouch. The little boy loved his toys and didn't go anywhere without the bear, his favorite. In 1922, while taking a morning break from playwriting, Milne innocently wrote a short poem about Christopher Robin saying his prayers. He didn't know at the time that this poem, called "Vespers," would brand him forever as a writer for children. As he later said, "It is easier in England to make a reputation than to lose one."[20]

For Better or Verse

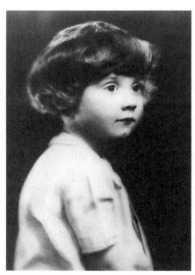

Milne's son Christopher Robin, after whom he named his stories' main character.

Believing the poem to be merely a sweet glimpse into the life of a child, Milne gave it to Daphne as a gift and told her she could publish it if she wanted. "Vespers" soon appeared in *Vanity Fair* magazine. It became so popular that it was reprinted as a wall hanging and hung in toddlers' nurseries around the world. Later, Christopher Robin would grow to resent the poem when the kids at school teased him. He even smashed the recorded version of it in a fit of anger.

As a result of "Vespers," Milne was asked to write another verse for children for a new magazine. He said he really wasn't interested in writing for children, but in 1923, during a rainy summer vacation, he decided to try the assignment. He quickly wrote a short, silly poem called "The Dormouse and the Doctor," and then just kept writing. By the time the boring holiday was over, he had written eleven sets of verses. A year later, he had enough for a book. The collection of poems was published in November 1924 under the title *When We Were Very Young*. It was illustrated by Ernest H. Shepard, an artist Milne knew from *Punch*. The dedication read, "To CHRISTOPHER ROBIN MILNE or, as he prefers to call himself, BILLY MOON, this book which owes so much to him is now humbly offered."[21]

In eight weeks, much to Milne and his publisher's astonishment, the book sold over fifty thousand copies. Some of the poems were set to music, and the songbooks were published only three weeks after the book. The *New York Telegraph* announced "Everybody's Talking about this Book," and the *Retail Bookseller* reported that sales of *When We Were Very Young* were "without parallel for any book in the last ten years."[22]

Comparisons with Lewis Carroll's *Alice's Adventures in Wonderland* flowed. After quoting one of Milne's poems, one reviewer wrote, "As [these poems] fall upon the ears of Alice in her wonderland she must know that a new prophet has arisen." Another wrote that "when A. A. Milne wrote *When We Were Very Young* he did more than write a book of adorable nonsense. He became an institution. As quotable, contagious and personal an institution as Lewis Carroll."[23] The poems are flawless in general composition, and according to Milne himself, "*When We Were Very Young* is not the work of a poet becoming playful, nor of a lover of children expressing his love, nor of a prose-writer knocking together a few jingles for the little ones, it is the work of a light-verse writer taking his job seriously."[24]

In 1925, Milne was asked to write a children's story for the Christmas Eve edition of the London newspaper the *Evening News*. Daphne suggested he write one of the bedtime stories he told Christopher Robin. Milne took her advice and wrote a story about the boy and his favorite stuffed bear, and constant companion, Winnie-the-Pooh.

Winnie-the-Pooh

The short story based on Christopher Robin and Pooh was published on the front page of the *Evening News* and was broadcast

Milne and Christopher Robin shortly after the publication of the first Winnie-the-Pooh *book.*

on the radio on Christmas Day. Milne realized he could write a whole book about Christopher Robin and his toys. After all, most of the characters were right in front of him, living upstairs in his son's nursery.

He began by writing short stories about the adventures in the Hundred Acre Wood of Pooh, a "Bear of Very Little Brain"; a gloomy donkey called Eeyore; a maternal kangaroo and her energetic baby (Kanga and Roo); a seemingly wise owl named Owl; a small, timid pig named Piglet; bossy Rabbit; and a little boy named Christopher Robin who watched over them. Bouncy Tigger didn't appear until some years later, because the real Christopher Robin hadn't been given him yet. Milne based the animals' personalities on the appearance of the real toys: "Their owner by constant affection had given them the twist in their features which denoted character. . . . They were what they are for anyone to see; I described rather than invented them. Only Rabbit and Owl were my own unaided work."[25] Three elements went into the writing of the book: Milne's nostalgia for his own beloved childhood, details from his son's current childhood, and the idealized version of childhood from his imagination. These elements, once combined, wove magic.

Milne collected the stories into one volume and again asked Ernest Shepard to illustrate them. Shepard happily went to Milne's home to draw the stuffed animals and to sketch Christopher Robin. In the end, he captured their likeness with amazing clarity, although he later admitted that Pooh looked more like his own son's teddy bear. Aware of the important role Shepard's illustrations played in the book, Milne decided that, instead of a flat payment, he would split the royalties with him 80/20. This was practically unheard of at the time.

Winnie-the-Pooh was published in 1926 to rave reviews such as: "Almost never has there been so much funniness in a book," "Mr. Milne has repeated the rare coup. Once more he has written the perfect book for children," and this one from the *New York Herald Tribune*: "As you read, the conviction grows on you that Mr. Milne has done it again. There are not so very many books that, sitting reading all alone, you find yourself laughing aloud over. This is one of them. Here is nonsense in the best tradition . . . with the high seriousness about it that children and other wise people love."[26]

Pulitzer prize–winning writer and professor Alison Lurie says of the book's success:

> It was Milne's genius to have created, working from such apparently simple materials, these universal types, and to have constructed in a few acres of English countryside a

world that has the qualities both of the Golden Age of history, and legend, and the lost paradise of childhood—two eras that, according to psychologists, are often one in the unconscious mind.[27]

The world clamored for more children's stories from Milne. In response, he published another book of verse in 1927 called *Now We Are Six*, followed in 1928 by the sequel to *Winnie-the-Pooh* called *The House at Pooh Corner*. Their success was just as great as the other two, and his American publisher claimed, "I believe Milne's four books are better known throughout the breadth and length of this land than any children's book in modern times."[28]

In *The House at Pooh Corner*, Christopher Robin must surrender part of his childhood as he heads off to school. In the final passage Milne leaves his readers with a sense that the stories will live on but that there will be no more Pooh books. "So off they went together. But wherever they go, and whatever happens to them on the way, in that enchanted place on the top of the Forest a little boy and his Bear will always be playing."[29] Milne was anxious to leave the Hundred Acre Wood behind and return to his dramatic writing for adults. He had no idea that the characters from his four short books would take on fully realized lives of their own, all too quickly overshadowing the life of their creator.

After the death of his brother, Milne made a failing attempt to get back into serious writing.

That Darn Bear

After mourning the death of his brother (and only close friend) Ken in 1929, Milne began writing his adult material again. He was surprised and saddened to discover that anything he wrote was being compared to his children's books, and found lacking. Never one to take criticism well, Milne became quite angry at what he felt was a grave injustice. His son was also beginning to feel angry at the fame that was thrust upon him, and he pulled away from his parents. Christopher Robin later claimed, "It seemed to me, almost, that my father had got to where he was by climbing upon my infant shoulders, that he had filched from me my good name and had left me with nothing but the empty fame of being his son."[30] This accusation came years after Milne had stated, "All I have got from Christopher Robin is a name which he never uses, an introduction to his friends . . . and a gleam which I have tried to follow. I do not want C. R. Milne ever to wish that his names were Charles Robert."[31]

The demand for Milne's children's books was so high during World War II that his publisher couldn't find enough paper to print them on. In 1947, twenty years after the books were written, Milne sent Christopher Robin's original stuffed animals (insured for $50,000) on a cross-country tour of America and created an "authentic birth certificate" for them. He didn't want the animals to be restored or cleaned up in any way; rather, he wanted them to appear as if a little boy had just finished playing with them. On the birth certificate he wrote, "No explanation is needed for the world-weariness of Pooh and Eeyore. Time's hand has been upon them since 1921. That was a long time ago."[32] The tour was so successful, with people traveling hundreds of miles to see the toys, that Milne agreed they should remain in America. They are now on permanent display at the New York Public Library, even though England has tried valiantly to get them back.

For a while Milne's plays continued to be produced, but by the 1950s almost all of his adult material was out of print. In 1952, Milne suffered a serious stroke. An operation a few months later left him partially paralyzed and unable to walk. He was still able to speak and to write a little, but the stroke had stripped him of most of his capacity for joy. Seeming to have come to terms with his legacy at last, he wrote to a fan, "There was an intermediate period when any reference to [Pooh] was infuriating; but now such a nice comfortable feeling envelops [the bear] that I can almost regard him impersonally as the creation of one of my favorite authors."[33]

The Afterlife

Milne remained seriously ill for three more years, finally succumbing on January 31, 1956. Christopher Robin came to visit him only twice during the time he was ill, but Milne felt he had already lost his son long ago. Milne had always wanted to become immortalized as a writer, to leave something behind him when he went. There is no doubt now of his immortality. Within their child-centered universe, the Pooh books offer children a "reassurance, a sense of kindness and friendship, of the freedom of adventuring without the threat of harm, of being loved despite one's faults."[34]

As one writer noted, "In his creation of Pooh, [Milne] . . . proved himself one of the supreme myth-makers, for Pooh has proved to be one of those rare characters who develop an existence apart from the books in which they are born."[35] One act of Daphne's has certainly helped keep the characters alive: She sold the film and merchandising rights of the *Pooh* characters to the Walt Disney Company in 1961. Since then, Pooh has been a huge business, currently bringing in over $100 million annually. Many of Milne's relatives complained that Disney "Americanized" the characters and the stories too much. They hope that the Disney version will at least lead new generations of young readers back to the original source.

Since its publication, *Winnie-the-Pooh* has been translated into an astonishing thirty-two languages worldwide, with the Latin version (*Winnie ille Pu*, 1960) becoming the first foreign language book to appear on the *New York Times* best-seller list. Milne's

Milne, shortly before his death in 1956.

characters have been spun off into adult-themed books like Benjamin Hoff's *The Tao of Pooh* (1982), which blends East Asian philosophy with stories from the Pooh books to illustrate its principles. The characters are printed on everything from bedding and watches to toothbrushes and backpacks. Disney recently gained the rights to the classic Shepard characters as well, ensuring an even larger merchandising opportunity.

Milne was a very wealthy man at the time of his death, and much of his royalties support the Literary Fund in England and his alma mater the Westminster School. Decades before he died, Milne inscribed the following poem in illustrator Ernest Shepard's copy of *Winnie-the-Pooh:*

When I am gone
let Shepard decorate my tomb
and put (if there is room)
two pictures on the stone:
Piglet, from page a hundred and eleven
and Pooh and Piglet walking (157) . . .
and Peter, thinking that they are my own,
will welcome me to heaven.[36]

CHAPTER 3

C. S. Lewis

When I was ten, I read fairy tales in secret and would have been ashamed if I had been found doing so. Now that I am fifty I read them openly. [A boy] does not despise real woods because he has read of enchanted woods: the reading makes all real woods a little enchanted. This is a special kind of longing. The boy reading the fairy tale desires and is happy in the very fact of desiring.[37]

—C. S. Lewis

During his career, C. S. Lewis wrote more than forty books on literary history and religion, two hundred essays, and nearly eighty poems. But even Lewis knew that it was his seven children's books that would grant him immortality. Since their appearance in the 1950s, the *Chronicles of Narnia* have been the most popular fantasy series ever written. Equally beloved on both sides of the Atlantic, more than a million copies are still sold each year. The appeal of modern-day children being transported to a land of enchantment and adventure has not lessened over time, even though the genre is often imitated. In writing the Narnia books, Lewis paid homage to E. Nesbit and George MacDonald, his favorite fantasy writers. Every fantasy writer after Lewis pays homage to *him*.

To millions of children and adults, Narnia isn't merely an imaginary land created by a man in England. It is a symbol of the place they long to reach, where good triumphs over evil and everyone possesses a little magic. The stories have many layers of meaning, as every good fantasy story should. C. S. Lewis himself had many layers, as all good fantasy writers must.

Early Childhood Joy

Clive Staples Lewis was born in Belfast, Ireland, on November 29, 1898. His father, Albert, was a lawyer. His mother, Flora, was a mathematician and a clergyman's daughter. His parents had very different personalities, and Lewis once said, "From my earliest years I was aware of the vivid contrast between my mother's cheerful and tranquil affection and the ups and downs of my father's emotional life. This bred in me long before I was old enough to give it a name a certain distrust or dislike of emotion as something uncomfortable and embarrassing and even dangerous."[38] Even at a young age Lewis felt he was a lot like his father, though they were soon to grow apart.

Author Clive Staples Lewis as a child.

At four years old, Lewis insisted on being called "Jacksie," and he had long before bestowed the nickname "Warnie" upon his brother Warren. These names (Jacksie was sensibly shortened to Jack) would stick with both of them for the rest of their lives. Only three years older, Warnie was Lewis's constant companion and lifelong best friend. Even though he suffered from nightmares (and would for many years), Lewis's early days were spent joyfully. Because of the threat of tuberculosis, children at that time were kept inside during bad weather. Since it rained a lot in Belfast, Lewis and Warnie learned to enjoy their time indoors. An Irish nanny told them stories about leprechauns and ancient gods, and both parents read to them from the piles of books in the house. Once Lewis was able to read himself, he read everything he could find, a habit he never lost. He loved *Gulliver's Travels* by Jonathan Swift, *The Story of the Amulet* by E. Nesbit, and *Squirrel Nutkin* by Beatrix Potter. Later he read tales of adventure by Mark Twain, H. Rider Haggard's *King Solomon's Mines,* and Arthur Conan Doyle's *Sir Nigel.* Everything he read fired his imagination and became fuel for his later writing. Lewis said that there was no beauty around him as a very young child, except for what was found in books. It wasn't until Warnie constructed a toy garden out of the lid of a biscuit tin (covered in moss and garnished with twigs and flowers) that Lewis realized the power of nature and felt the first stirrings of joy: "As long as I live my imagination of Paradise will retain something of my brother's toy garden."[39] Lewis also learned to recognize a feeling that would play an integral role in his life. Too young to wander the countryside, he could only watch the faraway green hills from his window. This notion of longing for something unattainable set him on his spiritual quest.

When Lewis was seven, the family moved to a large, rambling house farther into the country. "The New House," Lewis wrote in his autobiography, "is almost a major character in my story. I am a product of long corridors, empty sunlit rooms, upstairs indoor silences, attics explored in solitude, distant noises of gurgling cisterns and pipes, and the noise of wind under the tiles."[40] The house also held a large wardrobe carved out of oak by the boys' grandfather. They used to hide inside it among the clothes and make up stories.

Now that they lived in the countryside, the boys were able to ride their bicycles through the open farm country when the weather was good. They were also given their own playroom where they immediately set out creating their own country. The boys made up stories and complete histories of their world, which

Lewis (left) and his brother Warren (right).

they named Boxen. Lewis's contribution was called Animal-Land, where animals were dressed in fine clothes and could talk. He was initially frustrated that he couldn't construct things like houses and ships out of cardboard because he (along with his father and brother) couldn't move the joints in his thumbs: "I was driven to write stories instead; little dreaming to what a world of happiness I was being admitted. You can do more with a castle in a story than with the best cardboard castle that ever stood on a nursery table."[41] The boys would work on their secret world for hours, and when Warnie was away at boarding school Lewis wrote letters to keep him abreast of what was happening in Boxen.

When Lewis was nine, tragedy struck. His mother was diagnosed with cancer. His father didn't handle the situation well, and the boys drew closer to each other and further from him. When his mother died a few months later, Lewis felt like he had lost both parents. Deeply traumatized at this sudden turn of events, he said, "With my mother's death all settled happiness, all that was tranquil and reliable, disappeared from my life."[42]

The Price of Knowledge

Only a few days after his mother's death, Lewis was shipped off to school in England with Warnie. He hadn't known what to expect because Warnie rarely spoke of school when he was home on vacations. Lewis was shocked to discover that the headmaster of the school was a tyrant who didn't seem to care if the students learned anything at all. It was difficult enough for him to adjust to England itself, and he was miserable. Every time he went home for a short vacation, he dreaded going back: "The putting on of the school clothes was, I well knew, the assumption of a prison uniform."[43] Fortunately, the school soon closed. Lewis returned home for a short while and attended school locally. He later looked on this time fondly because he and his father grew close again. It was not to last, however, and he was sent back to England to a prep school named Cherbourg, where he would remain until he was nearly fifteen. Lewis enjoyed most of his time there and was inspired by some wonderful teachers. He discovered Norse legends in the book *Siegfried and the Twilight of the Gods* and fell in love with all things "Northern," including the music of Wagner inspired by the Norse tales.

Lewis's next school was nearby Malvern, which he approached with excitement. That excitement would immediately turn to fear and anxiety as he realized the older boys were terribly cruel to the younger ones. Sports were the school's number one concern, and

Lewis (right) and his brother (left) at home with their father, Albert.

Lewis never enjoyed them. He took refuge in the library, the one place where the younger students were safe from the whims of the older ones. When Lewis wrote about his school experiences in his autobiography, he used fictitious names to protect the guilty. The only thing that made this time bearable was stumbling into a friendship with Arthur Greeves, a boy back in Ireland. Lewis was astonished to learn that Arthur loved reading the same books of myth and legend that he did; he would be one of the most important people in Lewis's life for the next fifty years. After a year at Malvern Lewis begged his father to take him out of school, and finally his father agreed. He was sent to live and study under the private tutelage of W. T. Kirkpatrick (Kirk) in Great Bookham in Surrey, England. The two glorious years spent with Kirk made a scholar out of Lewis. Besides teaching him literature, philosophy and Greek, Kirk taught him to think deeply and to express his thoughts clearly. During that time a chance reading of George MacDonald's *Phantastes* awakening in Lewis a feeling of "holiness," a great baptizing of his imagination that was never to leave him.

Lewis earned a scholarship to Oxford, and when he arrived he told his father the college "surpassed my wildest dreams; I never saw anything as beautiful."[44] He was only there a short while, however, before being called to fight in World War I. In September 1917, he was commissioned as second lieutenant in the Somerset Light Infantry and sent to France. He arrived at the front lines on his nineteenth birthday.

A Scholar Emerges

After fighting for a few months, Lewis was hospitalized with trench fever. After he recovered, he was sent back to the front lines. His playful imagination helped him brave these tough times, as reflected in a letter to Warnie: "Today is wet—an outside world of dripping branches and hens in the mud and cold, which I am glad to have shut out. . . . How nasty the sugar cottage in *Hansel and Gretel* must have been in wet weather."[45] Only a few months later he was badly wounded and hospitalized again, this time in England. Feeling lonely, he asked his father to come visit him. But Albert was too stuck in his routine to take the trip, and Lewis was very hurt by this perceived abandonment.

Although he had shrapnel in his chest for the rest of his life, he felt lucky to be alive. Some of his close friends weren't as fortunate. He had made a pact with one of them, a fellow Irishman named Paddy Moore, that if either of them were killed, the other would watch over his family. Lewis kept this bargain and took up residence with Paddy's mother, Janie Moore, and her daughter Maureen. He would share a house with Mrs. Moore until her death over thirty years later.

Lewis returned to Oxford in January 1919 and quickly set about distinguishing himself at school. During his undergraduate years he won three of the major academic honors, an unheard-of accomplishment. He even published a book of lyric poems called *Spirits in Bondage* while only in his first year. Upon graduation, he wrote to his father, "I am quite sure that an academic or literary career is the only one in which I can hope ever to go beyond the meanest mediocrity. The Bar is a gamble . . . and in business of course I should be bankrupt or in jail very soon."[46] Fortunately, he landed a teaching position easily.

In 1924, Lewis began a one-year position as a philosophy professor at University College, Oxford. The following year he became a lecturer and tutor at Oxford's Magdalen College, specializing in English language and literature. He would hold this position for thirty years. In 1926 he wrote a book-length narrative poem called *Dymer* and became close friends with a group of fellow professors, including J. R. R. Tolkien, future author of *The*

Hobbit and *The Lord of the Rings,* and Owen Barfield, his closest friend from college. This group of scholars eventually called themselves the Inklings and met to discuss their various works-in-progress.

In 1929, Lewis's father died. Lewis had taken care of him during his decline, and was glad to have had that time together. The next year he and Mrs. Moore moved into a house only a few miles away from the college. They named it the Kilns, and soon his brother, Warnie, joined them there. During his twenties, Lewis was grappling with his religious beliefs. He tried hard to dismiss the idea of Christianity and organized religion, but in 1931, he became a Christian. He originally called himself "the most dejected and reluctant convert in all England."[47] This was soon to change as he embraced his newfound relationship with religion and wrote many best-selling books on the topic. One of these, *The Screwtape Letters* (a fictional correspondence between two devils published in 1942), is considered Lewis's most popular book, although he never considered it his best. It was so successful that he set up a fund directing two-thirds of his royalties on that and future projects to charity.

In the following years he lectured over the BBC radio (which would later form his book *Mere Christianity*); for a time his voice was as recognizable in England as Winston Churchill's. Meanwhile, he had continued to publish highly acclaimed scholarly works such as *The Allegory of Love: A Study in Medieval Tradition* in 1933 and *The Personal Heresy: A Controversy* in 1939, which sealed his growing reputation as one of the most brilliant scholars of the day.

In the 1940s Lewis produced a trilogy of popular science fiction novels for adults, all having a Christian bent to them. By this time his fame was spreading across the Atlantic, and in 1947, his face appeared on the cover of *Time* magazine in America. It was during the period that he began thinking about writing a book for children and dusted off some images that had been swirling around in his imagination for decades.

The Lion, the Witch, and the Wardrobe

"The *Lion* all began with a picture of a Faun carrying an umbrella and parcels in a snowy wood," wrote Lewis. "This picture had been in my mind since I was about sixteen. Then one day . . . I said to myself, 'Let's try to make a story about it.'"[48] Lewis had had very little contact with children until World War II brought them to him. He, Warnie, and Mrs. Moore housed evacuees from London whose parents wanted them farther out in the country. Usually awkward around children, Lewis began to enjoy and respect them more. One child asked about the wardrobe, and suddenly he had a story idea of four siblings walking through a wardrobe into another world. He jotted down notes but didn't do anything with them for nine more years. Encouraged by his friend and fellow writer Roger Lancelyn Green, he finally transferred the image of the faun in his head onto the page and into Narnia. The four siblings came along too, accompanied by a beautiful but evil witch, friendly talking animals, and a magnificent lion named Aslan. He read the first few chapters aloud to Green, who later said, "As he read, there had crept over me a feeling of awe and excitement: not only that it was better than most children's books which were appearing at the time—but the conviction that I was listening to the first reading of a great classic."[49] Even though J. R. R. Tolkien wasn't very supportive of the project initially, Lewis decided to use the same artist who illustrated Tolkien's most recent book. Then only in her midtwenties, Pauline Baynes would eventually draw thousands of illustrations for the Narnia series, her images helping the stories come to life.

When *The Lion, the Witch, and the Wardrobe* was published in 1950, it was awarded the prestigious Lewis Carroll Shelf Award for its originality and grasp of childhood wonder. As one reviewer wrote, "The Stories are unforgettable not only for the excitement and suspense of the adventures but also for the strong emotions they describe so well, especially the deep despair and fear caused by death and the unspeakable joy when death is conquered."[50] Another believed that "Once [Lewis] finally recognized that he was primarily a storyteller, he composed *The Chronicles of Narnia* to recreate the atmosphere of 'joy' that animated his youth. The seven enchanting fantasies capture a child's wonder in a world where marvelous possibilities seem to lurk around every corner . . . and support [Lewis's] critical insight that literature helps us mythologize our lives."[51] Children from England and across America instantly loved the book and couldn't wait for more. They didn't have long to wait, because over the next six years Lewis published six more books in the *Chronicles of Narnia*.

Aftermath

After the Narnia books were published, Lewis was flooded with letters from children. He considered it his duty to respond to every one, and sometimes his correspondence with a single child lasted for years. He was always gracious and answered their questions seriously and with good humor. It became evident to him that some of the children were discovering Christian overtones in the stories. Once teachers and parents became aware of this, some felt uneasy about supporting the books. Lewis denied that the books were allegories, as some claimed, but he admitted that the overtones were not a coincidence. He explained that "a strict allegory is like a puzzle with a solution, and the Narnia books were meant to be more like a flower whose smell reminds you of something you can't quite place."[52] He believed that children should enter Narnia first with their hearts, and only later with their minds.

The wardrobe which inspired Lewis to write The Lion, the Witch, and the Wardrobe.

In 1952, Lewis met an American coincidentally named Joy, an award-winning poet seventeen years his junior. Born Jewish, she had converted to Christianity largely as a result of reading Lewis's work. She and her two sons visited Lewis when they were in England, and he grew fond of her. Her eight-year-old son Douglas was a little disappointed when he first met Lewis. He remembers thinking, "Here was a man who was on speaking terms with King Peter, with the Great Lion, Aslan himself. Here was the man who had been to Narnia; surely he should at least wear silver chainmail and be girt about with a jewel-encrusted sword-belt."[53]

In 1955, Lewis was elected professor of medieval and Renaissance literature at Magdalene College, Cambridge (not to be confused with Magdalen College, Oxford). After thirty years at Oxford, he had been repeatedly snubbed for advancement because of the petty politics and jealousy of some faculty members. In 1956, he and Joy married because she would soon be deported otherwise. Lewis was surprised to find himself falling deeply in love with her, and a year later they married again in a religious ceremony. His brother, Warnie, said, "Joy was the only woman whom Lewis had met who had a brain which matched his own in suppleness, in width of interest, in analytical grasp, and above all in humor and sense of fun."[54] The only downfall of his marriage was the distancing of his male friends, who could not seem to make friends with his wife. He always regretted the loss of these vitally important men.

The Sun Sets on Narnia

Lewis's blissful married life was not destined to last long. By the time of their second wedding, Joy had already developed bone cancer and was in and out of the hospital. She was well enough to travel to Greece in 1960, a trip she had always dreamed of and one that was to be Lewis's last voyage as well. Later that year, after only three years of marriage, she died. Lewis poured his anguish into a book called *A Grief Observed,* which he published under a pseudonym in 1961. He wrote in a letter, "To lose one's wife after a very short married life may, I suspect, be less miserable than after a long one. You see, I had not grown *accustomed* to happiness. It was all a 'treat.' I was like a child at a party. But perhaps earthly happiness, even of the most innocent sort, is I suspect, addictive."[55]

In 1963, Lewis was forced to resign from teaching due to illness. He had developed a painful, calcium-draining bone disease (today known as osteoporosis) and was grappling with kidney disease and a weak heart. He told Warnie that he had done everything he had wanted to do, and he was ready to go. On November 22, 1963, a week before his sixty-fourth birthday, C. S. Lewis died at home. He shared the day of his death with writer and philoso-

Lewis shortly before resigning from teaching in 1963.

pher Aldous Huxley and President John F. Kennedy. By the time the news of Kennedy's assassination reached England, much of the country was already grieving.

Lewis's life was a quest for joy, in its many forms. Once he found it along the way, he shared it with the world. A close friend describes the funeral:

> There was one candle on the coffin as it was carried out into the churchyard. It seemed not only appropriate but almost a symbol of the man and his integrity and his absoluteness and his faith that the flame burned so steadily, even in the open air, and seemed so bright, even in the bright sun.[56]

Today the largest collection of Lewis's work is housed in the Wade Center at Wheaton College in Illinois. More than twenty-three hundred letters are available for the public to read, along with every book Lewis wrote, every book of his writings compiled and published after his death, and hundreds of books written *about* him. Tolkien, who outlived his friend by a decade, once joked that Lewis "will be the only author who published more books after he died."[57] Every year thousands of people—scholars, religious followers, and children—flock to the center to view the collection. Besides the written material, upon his death, Warnie Lewis donated his brother's writing desk, his fountain pen, and a favorite mug. But according to the proprietor of the center, "the big draw is the Wardrobe. Seven feet high and four feet across, it contains period-piece fur coats. A plaque playfully warns: 'Enter at your own risk. The Wade Center assumes no responsibility for persons who disappear or who are lost in this wardrobe.'"[58]

Lewis's life and the Narnia books continue to live on in many forms. New editions of the books are constantly being released, now with color illustrations and presented in chronological order according to the way Lewis agreed they should be read, rather than in the order he originally wrote them. The books have been dramatized as stage plays, live-action and animated movies, radio broadcasts, and books on tape. The story of Lewis's relationship with his wife, Joy, was made into two successful movies and a stage play, all called *Shadowlands*. The films took quite a bit of liberty with the facts, but Lewis's goodness and good humor still shone through. When President George Bush was looking for a campaign slogan, he found it in the sixth book in the *Chronicles of Narnia, The Magician's Nephew*. "A thousand points of light" actually refers to the creation of Narnia by Aslan. It also refers to the legacy C. S. Lewis left behind him when his one candle finally went out.

CHAPTER 4

E. B. White

Anyone who writes down to children is simply wasting his time. You have to write up, not down. . . . Some writers for children deliberately avoid using words they think a child doesn't know. [But] children are game for anything. I throw them hard words, and they backhand them over the net.[59]

—E. B. White

E. B. White wrote only three books for children in his nearly sixty-year writing career. He published more than two thousand essays and poems in magazines, newspapers, and books, and was recognized in his day as one of America's finest writers. As the *New Yorker* so aptly put it, his words were "so plain and so clearly pleasurable—a glass of cool water, a breeze on one's face."[60] When this great writer turned his pen toward writing books for children, he proved that kids deserved books as well written as any for adults. Literary critics contend that he has bestowed a great gift to children, and many consider *Charlotte's Web* to be the classic American children's book of the twentieth century. In a letter to a classroom of students, White himself summarizes his three children's books with his trademark simplicity and clarity: "*Stuart Little* is about the quest for beauty; *Charlotte* is a story of friendship, life, death, salvation; and *The Trumpet of the Swan* is a love story."[61] These basic truths are what make his books so special, and what makes his life so interesting. A shy and nervous man, he used a typewriter to tell the world what was inside him.

The Wonder Years

Elwyn Brooks White was born to Samuel and Lillian White on July 11, 1899, in Mount Vernon, New York. He was the youngest of six children in a rowdy and loving household. His father had quit school at thirteen and then worked his way up the ladder until he ran a piano manufacturing company. The family lived very comfortably in a large house that seemed to White like a protective fortress. From early on, he was a worrier.

> I was uneasy about practically everything: the uncertainty of the future, the dark of the attic, the . . . discipline of school, the transitoriness of life, the mystery of the church and God, the frailty of the body, the sadness of afternoon, the shadow of sex, the distant challenge of love and marriage, the far-off problem of a livelihood. I brooded about them all, lived with them day by day.[62]

White's childhood experiences greatly influenced the kind of person he would grow up to be. While still in grammar school he developed a fear of public speaking that was to remain with him for the rest of his life. He would be filled with dread at the thought of potentially embarrassing himself in front of his classmates, and on one occasion when he was chosen to recite a poem, he froze in the middle from terror and ran off the stage.

The White family portrait with the infant E. B. (center).

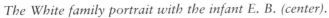

Even though he was fearful and shy, he had many wonderful, positive childhood experiences that became the foundations for his writing. He inherited his love of animals from his mother, and he recalls his joy and pride at watching three baby chicks hatch after he had taken care of the eggs. His beloved dog Mac was a constant companion, and throughout his life he enjoyed having dogs as pets. A small and thin boy, White didn't care much for organized sports. He loved doing tricks on his bicycle, canoeing at his family's summer house in Maine, and ice-skating in the winters at a local pond with a girl named Mildred. He reported that "this brief interlude on ice, in the days of my youth, had a dreamlike quality, a purity, that has stayed with me all my life. . . . I remember what it was like to be in love before any of love's complexities or realities or disturbances had entered in, to dilute its splendor and challenge its perfection."[63]

White began keeping a journal at eight years old. Writing became a way of calming himself down, since it allowed him to collect his thoughts. He explains that "A blank sheet of paper holds the greatest excitement there is for me. . . . I can remember . . . looking a sheet of paper square in the eyes when I was seven or eight years old and thinking, 'This is where I belong, this is it.'"[64] He taught himself to type on his older brother's typewriter and tried to learn as many interesting words as he could from the dictionary. In 1910 a poem he wrote about a mouse was published in the *Ladies' Home Companion,* and the next year he won a contest for his story "A Winter Walk," which was published in a popular journal for children called *St. Nicholas Magazine.* These accomplishments helped convince him he had talent, and he spent a great deal of his free time writing stories and poems about animals and life around him. He did well in school, but his motivation was mostly to keep up with his classmates and to avoid punishment by his teachers.

By the time White was in high school, he became very socially conscious. He wrote essays for the school magazine (of which he became an assistant editor) about how America should stay out of the impending World War I. Even though he was against it, when America did enter the war, White wanted to support his country's efforts. He was still too young to be drafted and was judged too skinny to join the army, so he spent his last summer before college working on farms whose owners had gone to fight. During this time between high school and college White thought a lot about what he should be doing with his life. On his eighteenth birthday he wrote, "My birthday! Eighteen and still no future! I'd be more contented in prison, for at least I would know precisely what I had to look forward to."[65]

Coming Out of His Shell

White's first year at college was spent mostly writing for the school paper—one of only two in America that was published daily. He still felt guilty about being in school instead of fighting the war, but he decided if he wasn't going to be selected, then he would do his best at college. He was trying hard to overcome his shyness and joined a fraternity. His new friends nicknamed him "Andy" since he shared his last name with the president of the university—Andrew White. White enjoyed having this nickname; in fact, many people called him Andy for the rest of his life. His social life was blooming, and he finally had the courage to start dating. During his junior year he was elected president of his fraternity and named editor-in-chief of the paper.

White was very influenced by one of his English professors, William Strunk Jr., who taught him the adage, "Each sentence you write is like a boat. One extra word can sink it."[66] White took this advice to heart, and simplicity and clarity became the goals of his writing. Nearly forty years later White would honor this great teacher by revising and publishing the professor's small textbook on writing, *The Elements of Style,* which is still considered the finest book on the rules of writing in existence. By the time of White's graduation in 1921, he had published over 180 editorials in the paper and was looking forward to a bright future. But unable to stay at any job longer than a few months, White realized he wasn't quite ready for a job in the real world and needed to take some time off. A college buddy, Harold Cushman, was only too happy to offer his companionship.

The Road Trip

White packed up his prized Model T Roadster with only the bare necessities for life on the road. Of course a typewriter was one of them. He and Cushman set out on their great cross-country adventure with little money and no destination. They often camped out or simply slept on the side of the road, writing short pieces along the way to pay for food. Besides selling their writing, they found short-term odd jobs. Between the two of them they sold roach powder, worked on ranches and farms, played piano in a café, washed dishes, ran a concession stand at a carnival, and sanded a dance floor. Basically, they had the time of their lives. White later said, "I spent a solid year experimenting with idleness and finding out exactly what it was like to occupy myself with nothing at all over a wide range of the country."[67]

When the two men arrived in Seattle, White decided to stay. He became a reporter for the *Seattle Times*—a paper he called "very highbrow, very conservative, very rich, and entirely unreadable."[68] After nearly a year he and a lot of the staff were laid off. Relieved, he went looking for more adventure; he found it in the form of a six-week cruise to Alaska. White convinced the captain to hire him since he couldn't afford passage after the first leg of the trip. Although he loved the experience, when the ship docked again in Seattle, White knew it was time to go home. He spent the next year and a half unhappily writing for advertising agencies and living with his parents. Then a new publication hit the newsstands, and soon the whole country would be reading the words of E. B. White.

The New Yorker

White devoured the first issue of the *New Yorker* and found it to be sophisticated and literary, yet a humorous and cheerful magazine. It focused on local New York issues as well as nationwide events, and White immediately sent in some essays. Within three months his first piece was published, and White moved from his parents' house into Greenwich Village. He soon began working for the magazine on a steady basis, editing and writing a column called "Notes and Comments." He would continue to work with the *New Yorker* in some capacity until the very last years of his life. His reputation as an insightful, humorous, and prolific writer grew. The mayor of New York City claimed he read every word White wrote, and supposedly President Coolidge did too. White was very modest about his own writing and jokingly explained that "The essayist is a self-liberated man, sustained by the childish belief that everything he thinks about, everything that happens to him, is of general interest. . . . Only a person who is congenitally self-centered has the effrontery and the stamina to write essays."[69]

The year 1929 was a big one for White, for both his career and his personal life. A collection of his poetry, *The Lady Is Cold,* was published to great reviews, and he and fellow writer James Thurber published a humorous book called *Is Sex Necessary?* Most important, White married *New Yorker* editor and longtime friend Katharine Angell. Making decisions was always problematic for White, but he called his marriage "The most beautiful decision of my life."[70] In 1931, they had a son they named Joel,

E.B. White and his wife Katharine.

which White was thrilled about. Katharine had two children from a previous marriage, and the children loved spending time together. Seven years later, the White family moved from New York to a farm near the coast of Maine. Now White could have animals around him again and his son could grow up in a more relaxed setting. From Maine, he continued to write for both the *New Yorker* and *Harper's* magazine, and Katharine continued to edit. In 1939, White recalled a dream he had a decade earlier about a "small character who had the features of a mouse, was nicely dressed, courageous, and questing."[71] This dream character would begin a new chapter in White's life, and it would change the course of children's literature forever.

Writing for Children

With one child of his own and eighteen nieces and nephews, White was always called on to tell stories. He discovered it was easier if he wrote them down first. One character appeared for many years—a little boy who was also a mouse who had many adventures. White began writing a full-length book about the mouse, who he named Stuart Little. It was hard for him to focus on such a lengthy endeavor, and he admitted he was "unable to sit still for more than a few minutes at a time, untouched by the dedication required for sustained literary endeavor, yet unable *not* to write."[72] After a move back to New York City in 1944, White put all his effort into finishing the novel.

In 1945, *Stuart Little* was published by Harper and Brothers under the editorial leadership of the famous editor Ursula Nordstrom. It sold 100,000 copies its first year. An illustrator named Garth Williams added nearly ninety pictures to the text, which White felt greatly attributed to the success of the book. White explained that Stuart's "quest for the bird Margalo symbolizes the continuing journey that everybody takes in search of what is perfect and unattainable. This is perhaps too elusive an idea to put into a book for children, but I put it in anyway."[73]

The mouse-boy caused quite a stir among some critics, who thought it was wrong to have children believe that a mouse could be born to human parents. Children themselves, though, had no problem understanding that the book was a fantasy. One influential librarian, Anne Carroll Moore, suggested that the book be withdrawn because the ending doesn't tie up the story, thereby never bringing the important sense of satisfaction to its child readers. Regardless of these criticisms, the book was a huge success, and at forty-six years old, E. B. White had embarked on the career that would make him world famous.

Spotlight on *Charlotte's Web*

When *Charlotte's Web* was first published in 1952, it received immediate critical and popular acclaim, and it was the runner-up for the Newbery Medal. It prompted the famous New York publisher (and editor of Dr. Seuss) Bennett Cerf to proclaim, "It is simply a perfect book. . . . If there is any book of the current season still in active circulation fifty years from now, it will be *Charlotte's Web*."[74] So far, history has shown he is correct. A nationwide poll of children and teachers taken in 1990 listed *Charlotte's Web* as the favorite book of kids across the country. The story about a spider who spins words into her web to save the life of a pig was unlike anything that came before it. After reading *Charlotte's Web*, writer and literary critic Eudora Welty wrote,

> What the book is about is friendship on earth, affection, and protection, adventure and miracle, life and death, trust and treachery, pleasure and pain, and the passing of time. As a piece of work it is just about perfect, and just about magical in the way it is done. What it all proves [as

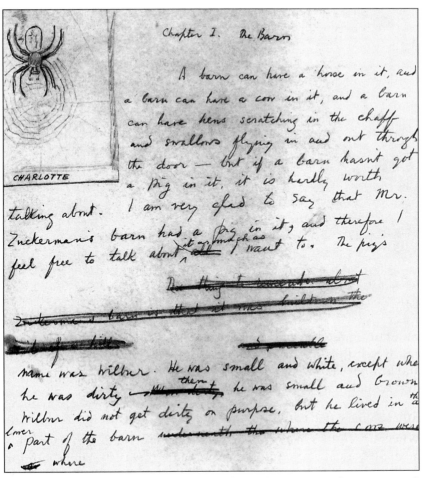

An early version of the manuscript for White's most famous novel, Charlotte's Web.

one of White's character's says in the book] is that human beings must always be on the watch for the coming of wonders.[75]

Before White sat down to write *Charlotte's Web*, he did nearly a year of research on spiders and animal behavior, wanting to be sure he got every detail exactly right. He drew sketches of the barnyard and rewrote the beginning of the story nine times until he was happy with it. His knowledge of farming and his love of animals gave him the foundation for the story, which he wrote from his tiny boathouse in Maine. By including the character of Fern, the little girl who saves Wilbur's life the first time it is threatened, White

The farm house from which the setting of Charlotte's Web *was taken.*

firmly places the story in the real world and gives the book another layer of depth.

Once again, Garth Williams illustrated the book, much to White's pleasure. It took them a while to agree on the appearance of Charlotte herself, but eventually they were both happy with it. One literary critic said that "*Charlotte's Web* is a collaboration of text and picture, in which Garth Williams has his own things to say."[76] The book was not pushed out of the number one spot on the *New York Times* best-selling children's books list until 1970, when White's new (and last) book for children, *The Trumpet of the Swan*, temporarily bumped it to number two.

Glory

With the publication of *Charlotte's Web,* White's fame grew to a level perhaps unsurpassed by any other contemporary American writer. In 1958, he was awarded the illustrious Lewis Carroll Shelf Award, and in July 1963, he received a telegram from President John F. Kennedy announcing he had been awarded the Presidential Medal of Freedom for his contribution to the quality of life in America. This is the highest honor an American can receive in a time of peace. The president called him an essayist whose concise comment on men and places had revealed to yet another age the vigor of the English sentence. White felt very honored by this award and said, "Finding myself on [Kennedy's] list was the most gratifying thing that ever happened to me, as well as a matter of pride and sober resolve."[77]

White was awarded the prestigious Laura Ingalls Wilder Award for his contribution to children's literature in 1970, the same year *The Trumpet of the Swan* hit the shelves. He wasn't as pleased with this novel as he had been with the other books, both of which had been made into successful television and movie projects. Although happy with the illustrations, he felt bad that Garth Williams could not do them because he was at work on another project. He also said, "I'm not entirely happy about the text of the book—I am old and wordy, and this book seems to show it."[78] But like the last two, it was quickly embraced by children and the awards continued to flow.

In 1971 White won the National Medal for Literature, and in 1978 he was given a special Pulitzer prize for his variety of writing for many years. As was his manner, he never made a big deal over any of his awards, and he still refused to give acceptance speeches. His demand for privacy grew even stronger in his later years, especially after his wife died in 1977. He retired to the farm and kept his life simple—tending the animals, canoeing every once in a while, and visiting with his grandchildren.

E. B. White, soon after being awarded the National Medal for Literature.

53

A Literary Life Ends

When E. B. White died on October 1, 1985, at the age of eighty-six, one reporter wrote, "He made us laugh and he made us cry, and we are the richer for it."[79] His stepson Roger, a distinguished writer in his own right, joked that White would have avoided his own funeral if he could have. In White's essays his "usual subject was the world as he saw it with his eyes open, his gaze clear and analytical. [His children's books] report on the world as it was understood by his heart."[80] Nowhere is that more apparent than when Charlotte dies alone at the end of *Charlotte's Web* and even the toughest heart can't help but weep.

CHAPTER 5

Dr. Seuss

I like nonsense. It wakes up the brain cells. Fantasy is a necessary ingredient for living. It's a way of looking at life through the wrong end of a telescope, which is what I do. And that enables you to laugh at all of life's realities. . . . I am just saying to kids that reading is fun.[81]

—Dr. Seuss

Dr. Seuss has sold more children's books than any other author in the world. He revolutionized how children learn to read and created the concept of the "easy reader" book. His playful text and outrageous illustrations are so carefully enmeshed that each one is a perfect counterpart to the other. In forty-seven books, Dr. Seuss celebrated the individual and the extraordinary in the ordinary, and he turned generations of kids into lifelong fans. He gave his audience a sense of self-confidence, jump-started their imagination, and bestowed upon them an appreciation of others and of the world around them. "I've published great writers," said his editor Bennett Cerf. "Everyone from William Faulkner to John O'Hara. But there's only one genius on my authors' list. His name is Ted Geisel."[82] And Ted Geisel is the real Dr. Seuss.

The Early Years

Dr. Seuss was born Theodor Seuss Geisel in Springfield, Massachusetts, on March 2, 1904. His parents, Theodor Robert and Henrietta, were both of German descent, and Geisel grew up learning both German and English. He had an older sister, Marnie, who he loved playing with and a younger sister, Henrietta, who died of pneumonia before she was two. The family was very close, and both of Geisel's parents encouraged their children to learn about life and to explore. They went to the beach every summer and to the town library whenever

Geisel wanted to feed his hungry appetite for books. He loved the *Rover Boys* series and read thirty in a row. Before he was ten he read adult books and spent much of his free time doodling. Inspired by animals he saw at the zoo, he would come home and draw his own animals, which usually didn't bear much resemblance to the real ones. His mother, one of his early fans, occasionally let him draw on the attic walls. Even at a young age he drew odd-looking people and bizarre animals whom he gave odd and bizarre names. Not many people besides his family appreciated his artwork, however. In

Young Theodor Seuss Geisel, known to millions as Dr. Seuss.

his only art class—in high school—his teacher told him, "You'll never learn to draw, Theodor. Why don't you just skip this class for the rest of term?"[83]

Geisel considered his father his role model. He thought he was a perfect example of perseverance. After his brewery was shut down during Prohibition (when producing, selling, and consuming alcohol became illegal), his father took over as the chairman of the town's parks commission, a position he had held as a volunteer for years. Geisel was proud of his father and always wanted his father to be proud of him. It was his mother who instilled in Geisel his love of language, however, and he believes the rhythm with which she read him bedtime stories was responsible for the beat and tempo of his writing.

When World War I began in 1914, it was hard to be of German descent in America. Geisel was taunted at school but tried very hard to rise above it. On one hand he was shy and unassuming, but by the time he was in high school he had a reputation for his sense of humor and his creativity. Even though his father was always trying to make an athlete out of him, he chose instead to write for the school newspaper and even acted in a few school plays. He still harbored a love of reading, and in his senior year he discovered a writer he claimed gave him his love of the hypnotic power of rhyme—Hilaire Belloc, author of *The Bad Child's Book of Beasts*.

When Geisel set off for college at Dartmouth, he had no idea what direction his life would take. In hindsight, though, he had been preparing for his line of work since he could hold a pencil. His strange characters and sense of humor kept bringing him back to the same place—making people laugh while making them think. It still took many years before he realized he could make a living at it.

A Blossoming Cartoonist

As soon as Geisel arrived at Dartmouth in the fall of 1921, he was immediately drawn to the college's infamous humor magazine, the *Jack O'lantern*. He wrote humorous articles and drew cartoons and quickly became known around campus. He majored in English, but his education definitely came second to the magazine. His one goal, to become editor-in-chief, was realized at the end of his junior year. A few months before graduation, however, the post was taken away from him after he and some friends were caught breaking the rules of Prohibition. But Geisel wouldn't let that stop him. He continued editing and contributing to the magazine but began signing his pieces with made-up names. It was at this time that he first began using the name Seuss (his mother's maiden name and his own middle name). The "Dr." would come later. With typical modesty, Dr. Seuss said that during his time at the *Jack O'lantern*,

> I discovered the excitement of "marrying" words to pictures. I began to get it through my skull that words and pictures were Yin and Yang. I began thinking that words and pictures, married, might possibly produce a progeny more interesting than either parent. It took me almost a quarter of a century to find the proper way to get [them] married. At Dartmouth I couldn't even get them engaged.[84]

After Dartmouth, Geisel headed to Oxford University in England to pursue a doctorate in literature. It didn't take him (or his professors) long to realize that his heart wasn't in it. Reviewing one of his notebooks, Geisel pointed out, "As you go through the notebook, there's a growing incidence of flying cows and strange beasts. And finally, at the last page of the notebook there are no notes on English Literature. There are just strange beasts."[85] After encouragement from a fellow student, Helen Palmer, he decided that the bizarre doodles that filled the margins of his notebooks were what he should really be pursuing. He also decided that he wanted Helen to be his wife and proposed before he dropped out of graduate school.

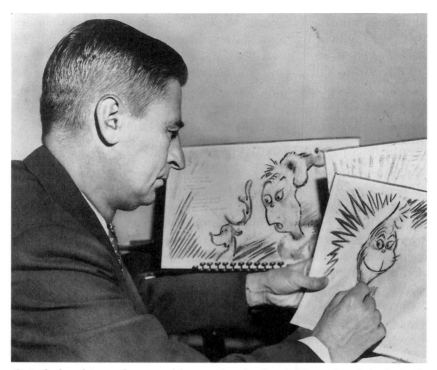

Geisel sketching what would soon be the book How the Grinch Stole Christmas.

After a trip through Europe and a short stint studying in Paris, the two returned to America. Helen began teaching in New Jersey, and Geisel moved back in with his parents in Massachusetts while he sent out cartoons to all the popular magazines. After many rejection slips, the *Saturday Evening Post* bought one of his cartoons for $25. On the heels of that success he moved to New York City and began working as a staff writer and artist at a magazine called *Judge.* In 1927, he and Helen finally had enough money to get married, and they moved into an apartment across from a stable where dead horses were often left out in the street until the sanitation department arrived days later to take them away. Because of financial problems at *Judge,* his salary was cut and he was often paid in products from the magazine's advertisers. Once he received a hundred cartons of Barbasol shaving cream and later 1,872 Little Gem nail clippers. Fortunately, other magazines were buying his work and paid in cash.

It was during this time that the rest of his pseudonym appeared. One of his projects at *Judge* was a series about animals called "Boids and Beasties." To make the pieces seem more credible, he added the "Dr." before his name. He still used Seuss in the hope that one day he'd write the "great American novel" using his real name. Soon after he got a job writing humorous ads for a popular insecticide called Flit and made enough money to move to a nice apartment, where, he said proudly, "there were many fewer dead horses."[86]

Finding His Voice

Geisel would work for the next seventeen years on the Flit campaign, and his slogan, "Quick, Henry, the Flit!" made the insecticide a household name. But after a few years of that he needed to find a way to bring more creativity into his life. He waited for inspiration to hit him, and when it did, in 1937, his wife encouraged him to pursue it. While they were traveling on a ship, the rhythm of the ship's engines sounded to him like someone saying, "and to think that I saw it on Mulberry Street." He wrote a story to go along with the sentence, and the resulting book was rejected by nearly thirty publishers. Then one day a very fortuitous meeting occurred. Geisel was walking along the street, the manuscript tucked under his arm, when he ran into an old college friend. His friend, who had just landed a job as an editor at Vanguard Press, inquired about his package. Within the day, Geisel had his first book contract, and soon *And To Think That I Saw It on Mulberry Street* was breaking sales records for children's books. Finally, there was a book for young readers that they could read on their own and it didn't have Dick, Jane, or Spot in it. As one literary scholar pointed out, "Such a fortunate meeting is the stuff of fantasy, an appropriate beginning for the career of Dr. Seuss."[87]

Geisel now had a mission. He wanted to revolutionize the way children were taught to read by showing them that reading can be fun. "There's been too much 'Come here, Fido,' in kids' readers," he said. "I sometimes wonder how any of us learned to read."[88] His unique style never wavered much from book to book. The text was almost always written in an infectious, repetitive form of verse called anapestic tetrameter. This consists of a metric foot made of two short unstressed syllables followed by a stressed syllable. There are four of these feet to each line. One of Geisel's best-loved characters is Horton the elephant, and these famous lines from *Horton Hatches the Egg* are a perfect example of anapestic tetrameter:

I meant what I said, and I said what I meant.

An elephant's faithful, one hundred percent.[89]

Geisel kept the text on every page very brief. When he couldn't come up with a rhyme, he simply made up words. The stories all have a swift pace, an unceasing momentum, in which the action builds and builds until children are literally bouncing in their seats in anticipation of the ending. By making his illustrations full of movement, he assured that the reader would keep turning the pages. His characters were bold, strong figures with simple lines, often placed in surreal settings. He used bright, unshaded primary colors and made sure that everything in the text was reflected in the art and vice versa. Geisel also ensured that the stories, outlandish as they were, had an inner logic. "If I start with a two-headed animal I must never waver from that concept. There must be two hats in the closet, two toothbrushes in the bathroom and two sets of spectacles on the night table. Then my readers will accept the poor fellow without hesitation and so will I."[90] With the onset of World War II, serious times were ahead for America, and Dr. Seuss found he had a lot to say about it.

The Moral of the Story

Between 1940 and 1947 Geisel was too involved in the war effort to continue writing his children's books. He joined the army and was sent to Los Angeles to write and produce war documentaries. During this time he won two Academy Awards for documentaries titled *Hitler Lives* and *Design for Death,* with one more to follow a few years later. In 1948, he and Helen settled in an oceanfront house in La Jolla, California, where they converted the top floor of an old watchtower on their property into Geisel's writing studio. Geisel's habit of "sliding a moral in sideways" in his books became even more evident in the ones he wrote after the war. He believed that "Kids can see a moral coming a mile off and they gag at it. But there's an inherent moral in any story."[91] "Children have a strong ethical sense anyway. They want to see virtue rewarded and arrogance or meanness punished. If the Grinch steals Christmas, he has to bring it back in the end. I must say, though, when I was doing that one, I was kind of rooting for the Grinch."[92] In *Horton Hears a Who* (1954), Geisel demonstrates the idea that everyone has the responsibility to look after everyone else, no matter how small they are. Later the "commercialization of Christmas is explored in *How the Grinch Stole Christmas* (1957); totalitarianism in *Yertle the Turtle;* pollution in the ecological allegory *The Lorax* (1971); discrimination in *The Sneetches and Other Stories* (1961); nuclear disarmament in *The Butter Battle Book* (1984)"[93]; and the cultivation of inner strength and perseverance in 1990's *Oh, the Places You'll Go.*

But alongside these "message books," Geisel continued to turn out a book a year simply celebrating whimsy, lyricism, and the limitless boundaries of a child's imagination. He wanted kids to know that they are unique and special, as demonstrated in books like *The Shape of Me* and *My Book About Myself.* The book that is his trademark and his own personal favorite gave birth not only to one very fun-loving cat but to the entire Beginning Reader Book industry.

The Cat in the Hat

It began with a challenge. In May 1954, author John Hersey wrote an article for *Life* magazine bemoaning the high illiteracy rate among America's children. He attributed it in part to the boring how-to-read textbooks and suggested that things might change if someone like Dr. Seuss were writing those books. The textbook editor (and later president) of Houghton Mifflin, the country's largest textbook publisher, was willing to give it a try. He sent Geisel a list of about three hundred vocabulary words from an approved beginning-reader-level list and told him to try to write a book using just those words. After sweating over the project, Geisel almost gave up. Then his eyes alighted on two words on the list that rhymed—cat and hat. Nine months later, 233 words were crossed off the list, the book was finished, and children's publishing (and Geisel's life) would never be the same again.

When *The Cat in the Hat* was published in 1957 it was an overnight success, selling more than any other hardcover book at that time. Children and adults loved the mischievous cat in the stovepipe hat who did all sorts of things that good little boys and girls weren't supposed to do. When the author of the *Life* magazine article read the book, he called it "a gift to the art of reading . . . a masterpiece."[94] At the end of his life, Geisel claimed that *The Cat in the Hat* was the book he was most proud of, because it brought an end to the Dick and Jane and Spot method of learning to read. The success of the book led Random House (which published the book for the general market) to launch a new publishing department called Beginner Books, aimed at creating books for the youngest reader (later an imprint for even younger children was created called Bright and Early Books). Geisel and his wife, Helen, headed up these new departments, which not only published Dr. Seuss's books like *Green Eggs and Ham* and *One Fish, Two Fish, Red Fish, Blue Fish,* but gave writers and illustrators like Stan and Jan Berenstain (*The Berenstain Bears* series) their

Dr. Seuss holding a copy of The Cat in the Hat.

start. "For thirteen years Ted was the editor of nineteen of our books," said the Berenstains upon Geisel's death in 1991. "Hardly a day passes that one or the other of us doesn't draw upon his wit, wisdom and joie de vivre [joy of life]."[95]

How the Grinch Stole Christmas was also published in 1957, and at the end of the year Random House totaled up the amount of fan mail addressed to Dr. Seuss. It weighed 9,267 pounds. Dr. Seuss was now a household name, and his fame only grew after the publication of *Green Eggs and Ham* in 1960. Still his best-selling book, it, too, was born from a challenge. After the success of *The Cat in the Hat,* Geisel's editor, Bennett Cerf, bet him $50 that he couldn't write a book using only a hundred different words. Geisel said he could do it with fifty words. Geisel won the bet, and the result, *Green Eggs and Ham,* is the seventh best-selling children's book in history.

Rooting for the Grinch

His license plate said "Grinch." He had been known to escape to the gambling halls of Las Vegas on his birthday rather than face the twenty thousand cards and packages of green eggs and ham that were sent from children all over the world. He claimed that if he were invited to a dinner party with his book characters, he wouldn't show up. But no one worked harder than Ted Geisel to create those characters. "I know my stuff all looks like it was rattled off in twenty-three seconds, but every word is a struggle, and every sentence is like the pangs of birth."[96] He sat at his desk at least eight hours a day (sometimes well into the night), and with only a few exceptions, it took him around a year to complete each book. He would write five hundred pages just to get a sixty-page book in the end. Ninety percent of his drawings got tossed out also. "I may doodle a couple of animals; if they bite each other, it's going to be a good book. If you doodle enough, the characters begin to take over themselves—after a year and a half or so."[97] When he was stuck and couldn't draw his way out, he would run up and down the stairs, put on strange hats, and lie on the floor for hours. Luckily, both his wives (he married Audrey Dimond after the death of Helen in 1967) understood his peculiar habits and encouraged him.

In 1984 he was presented with a Pulitzer prize for his contribution to the education and enjoyment of America's children. He never had any children of his own, but he was very close to his niece and to Audrey's children from her previous marriage. One of his favorite letters was one he received in the 1950s from a boy who wrote, "Dr. Seuss has an imagination with a long tail." When

Geisel signing books on Dr. Seuss Day at Dartmouth College.

Geisel read that, he commented, "That fellow will go places."[98] Over thirty years later, his last book, *Oh, the Places You'll Go,* was published. It became the longest-running children's book on the *New York Times* nonfiction best-seller list, and it often makes reappearances on the list each year around school graduation time. Always generous, Geisel founded the Dr. Seuss Foundation, which donates money to scholarships, libraries, charities, and zoos.

After suffering a heart attack and throat cancer (he was a chain smoker), Theodor Geisel died in his sleep on September 24, 1991, at age eighty-seven. Children and adults around the world mourned his passing. To celebrate his life and his contribution to reading, schools nationwide hold a "Read Across America" day each year on his birthday, when respected members of the local community visit schools to read and discuss his books. Geisel would have appreciated the statement one sad first-grade girl told a reporter upon learning of his death: "I would have liked to have told him that we're going to miss him, we love him, and we'll always remember him until the day he comes back alive."[99]

More than 200 million copies of Dr. Seuss's books have been sold; many have been made into Emmy-winning television specials; and most have been translated into more than twenty languages, despite the inherent difficulties with rhyming in foreign languages. Geisel won three Caldecott Honor Awards, two Lewis Carroll Shelf Awards, the Laura Ingalls Wilder Award, and dozens more. Each year the Dr. Seuss Picture Book Award gives money and a publishing contract to an aspiring illustrator.

Thousands of pieces of Geisel's original artwork and manuscripts are housed at the University of California in San Diego. Although he rarely agreed to license his characters during his lifetime, since his death they have taken on lives of their own. They've been turned into stuffed animals and board games and have been plastered on posters and t-shirts, socks, ties, and underwear. There's even a theme park at Universal Studios in Orlando, Florida, called Seuss Landing, with rides and activities based on the Dr. Seuss books.

With three out of the top ten best-selling children's books of all time, Geisel's contribution to the world of children's literature is colossal. An old friend and associate summed it up well: "Trying to remember Ted in a few words is like trying to cram a giant into a small bottle. This was a man who created a whole new world, a whole new way of viewing children's books, and in doing so he left a legacy of delight for all children, for all time."[100]

CHAPTER 6

Roald Dahl

Children are much more vulgar than grownups. They have a coarser sense of humor. They are basically more cruel.[101]

The writer for children must be a jokey sort of a fellow . . . he must like simple tricks and jokes and riddles and other childish things. He must be unconventional and inventive. He must have a really first-class plot.[102]

—Roald Dahl

Roald Dahl spent his life being unconventional. A man full of contradictions, he was at the same time philanthropic yet financially ambitious, macho and controlling yet childlike, brave, funny, and gentle. His childhood, equal parts joy and pain, became the foundation for his wildly successful children's books. As the director of the movie version of *James and the Giant Peach* said, "He invests his children protagonists with great imagination, which they use to face either monsters or evil adults, and to come up with preposterous ideas that turn out to work wonderfully."[103]

Roald Dahl's children's books are unique, and many consider them to be the most popular children's books in history. His authority figures are cruel and often meet macabre deaths, his child heroes are mischievous and powerful, his settings are bizarre and fantastical, and his tone is light and full of humor and nonsense. This mixture had never been seen before, and it is a rare author writing today who can equal it.

Tales of Childhood

Roald Dahl was born to Norwegian parents on September 13, 1916, in Llandaff, South Wales, Britain. When Dahl was three years old, his oldest sister, Astri, died from appendicitis, which devastated his father, Harald, a successful shipbroker (someone who supplies ships with everything they need). A year later Harald died when his grief overpowered his will to fight off pneumonia. He left his widow, Sofie, with five children (including two from his previous marriage) and a baby on the way. Sofie had promised to educate the children in English schools, so the family stayed in Wales instead of returning to her native Norway.

Dahl, an energetic, fun-loving boy, began his education at Llandaff Cathedral School, where he met with his first model of the cruel authority figure. His first beating resulted from a prank he pulled with a group of friends after a visit to the local candy shop. Their daily trip to the shop after school was the only thing that made school bearable. The owner of the shop, however, always yelled and taunted them as they handed over their pennies. One day they decided to get even with her. Dahl dropped a dead mouse into the jar of gobstoppers, and as a result, all the boys got cane-whipped by their headmaster while the candy shop owner cheered him on. Dahl's horrified mother decided to send him to boarding school the next year.

Dahl was glad to have escaped the Cathedral School, but he had no idea how homesick he would be at St. Peter's School. This was the first time he had been apart from his family, and he missed them very much. He wrote to his mother every Sunday, a tradition he continued religiously until she died thirty-two years later. In addition, Dahl soon discovered that the rules were even stricter at boarding school, and it was hard for him to avoid trouble. Later in life he said, "All through my school life I was appalled by the fact that masters and senior boys were allowed literally to wound other boys, and sometimes quite severely. I couldn't get over it. I never have got over it . . . [it has left] a lasting impression of horror upon me."[104] In order to give himself some small comfort at night, he would turn himself around in his bed until he was facing his family's house. He slept this way the entire time he was away at school.

Never a distinguished student, Dahl lived for the summer, when his entire family vacationed on a beautiful private island in Norway. It was a three-day trip that included boats and trains and exotic ports, and he loved every minute of it. By the time Dahl got to high school he had resigned himself to the fact that no matter what school he attended, the English educational system was cruel and degrading to children. He hated the fact that the older boys had unlimited power over the younger, and he refused to carry on that tradition (although he wasn't above verbal teasing). He tried to distract himself by staying busy. He read a lot and discovered he was good at sports. By playing on the school teams he was able to spend more time outside and away from the campus. He also developed a love for photography and built his own darkroom at school. His classmates and teachers were impressed with his artistic abilities, even if they weren't impressed with his scholastic ones. In fact, one English teacher said, "I have never met a boy who so persistently writes the exact opposite of what he means. He seems incapable of marshalling his thoughts on paper." Another said he was "a persistent muddler, his vocabulary was negligible, his sentences mal-constructed." Yet another said "this boy is an indolent and illiterate member of the class."[105] It is no wonder that after high school Dahl refused to go to college. He wanted to live by his own rules, see the world, and have adventures. He got exactly what he wished for.

Adventures

Dahl wanted a job where he would be stationed in a foreign land, and he surprised everyone by landing a very competitive position with Shell Oil. He loved wearing business suits and taking the train into London each day, but he was thrilled when he got a three-year assignment to East Africa. After a two-week boat trip, Dahl, at twenty-one years old, began his adventure. While supplying Shell's customers with oil, he learned Swahili, got malaria, shook scorpions out of his boots, met fascinating characters, lived among wild and dangerous animals, and went on safaris. He saved a man from being bitten by a deadly snake and witnessed a woman being snatched by a lion and then dropped, unharmed. In fact, he was asked to write about the incident with the lion for an African newspaper, which became his first published piece. "Above all," Dahl recalled years later, "I learned how to look after myself in a way that no young person can ever do by staying in civilization."[106]

Before his time in Africa was over, however, World War II began. Dahl joined the Royal Air Force (RAF) and trained along with sixteen other young men to be a fighter pilot. At six feet, six inches, it was a tight fit in the cockpit, but Dahl loved flying. On his very first mission in Libya, he was given incorrect information and crashed his plane into the desert. His nose was smashed in, his skull fractured, and he was blind for weeks. It took him five months at a navy hospital to recover from his injuries, and then he was sent back to fight. In Greece, he rejoined his squadron and learned that they were completely outnumbered by the Germans. Each day Dahl flew his tiny Mark I Hurricane over the beautiful

Mediterranean Sea, exchanged fire with the German planes, and was amazed to make it back to camp alive. He was then sent to Haifa, where blinding headaches forced him to return home. Of the sixteen pilots in his original training squadron, only three survived the war. One of the lucky ones, Dahl was about to begin a whole new career, one that would take him across the Atlantic and make him world famous.

A Writer Is Born

Since Dahl was medically unable to fly, the RAF sent him to America to work at the British Embassy. His job there was to report on America's war efforts. This position allowed him to meet important people and socialize with Washington high society. One day a famous English writer living in America named C. S. Forester came to see Dahl. He had heard of Dahl's plane crash and asked him if he could interview him for the *Saturday Evening Post*. Dahl was very excited to meet this hero of his and agreed to write up notes on the incident. When Forester read what Dahl wrote, he told him it was excellent and that he was a natural-born writer. This came as a great surprise to Dahl, who had never done well in English classes. The magazine published Dahl's story to great acclaim, and a writer was born.

For the next few years Dahl wrote fictional short stories based on his flying experiences, and they were all accepted at prestigious magazines. His first book for children, called *The Gremlins,* was published in 1943. The story, about tiny mischievous creatures who sabotaged airplanes, was almost made into a movie by Walt Disney. Even though it never came to fruition, Dahl enjoyed meeting Disney in Los Angeles and collaborating with him.

Dahl returned to England in 1945 having sold nearly twenty short stories for adults. Reviewers noted that "Generally macabre in nature, his stories won praise for their vivid details, carefully constructed plots, and surprise endings."[107] In the early 1950s, having earned his reputation as one of the leading short story writers of his day, he rented an apartment in New York City to be closer to the publishing industry. While there, he met movie star Patricia Neal at a party. They were married eight months later, on July 2, 1953. They kept an apartment in New York and bought an old farmhouse in England. It was there, in a tiny shed in the apple orchard, that Dahl did all his writing. Inside the cramped shed Dahl kept a sleeping bag for the cold, an old suitcase to prop up his feet, and, as his daughter recalls, "a ball of foil made from the wrappers of his weekly chocolate bar;

The wedding of Roald Dahl and Patricia Neal on July 2, 1953.

pieces of his own backbone [from an operation] floating in preservative, and a rock veined with opal sent to him by a young Australian fan."[108]

His daughter Olivia was born in 1954, followed by another daughter, Tessa, in 1957 and a son, Theo, in 1960. Dahl loved being a father, and every night he made up bedtime stories. One of the girls' favorites was about a giant peach. Growing frustrated with his short story writing, Dahl decided to turn his focus onto children and wrote *James and the Giant Peach.* (In the original version the giant peach was a giant cherry.) It took him almost nine months of reworking the story until he was satisfied. After reading the manuscript, publisher Alfred Knopf wrote, "I have just read with absolute delight your juvenile [book]. If this doesn't become a little classic, I can only say that I think you will not have been dealt with justly."[109] The book has, in fact, become a classic for reasons noted by the *Times Educational Supplement*: "Dahl had the ability to home unerringly in on the very nub of childish delight, with brazen and glorious disregard for what is likely to furrow the adult brow."[110] By the time *James and the Giant Peach* was published, Dahl had already written the first draft of a book he called *Charlie's Chocolate Boy*, a book that would soon propel him to superstardom.

Charlie and the Chocolate Factory

His new book about a poor boy chosen to visit a mysterious chocolate factory had to wait a few more years before it was eventually published in 1964. Dahl had two family tragedies to deal with first. At only four months old, his son Theo's stroller was hit by a New York City taxicab and his skull was fractured. Dahl did everything he could to help his son, even helping to invent a medical device to help drain fluid from his brain. Theo slowly recovered, but he would suffer permanent damage in that he was slow to learn. The family moved back to England. Just two years later, Dahl's oldest daughter, Olivia, died from a severe case of measles encephalitis. Dahl was overwhelmed with grief and thought he would never write again. Pat continued to get movie roles, and the family traveled with her while they mourned.

Finally Dahl forced himself back to work and completed the newly renamed *Charlie and the Chocolate Factory*. A lifelong lover of sweets, Dahl's idea for the story came from his own childhood. While he was in school, the Cadbury chocolate company used to send samples of their newest chocolate bars to the students for their opinions. Dahl had always wondered how the chocolate was made and used to fantasize about it. As for the owner of Dahl's fictitious factory, Willy Wonka, he bore a strong resemblance to his creator.

Dahl, shortly before the publication of Charlie and the Chocolate Factory.

The book, like most of his others to come, was published first in America. The print run of ten thousand copies sold out within a month (a few years later when it was published in China, its initial print run was 2 *million*). The book appealed to children because of its fantastical setting, strange characters, slapstick humor, and the idea that an ordinary boy like Charlie could achieve great things. Kids loved the rhymes and puns and the songs by the Oompa-Loompas. The book received its share of controversy as well as praise. Some critics thought the book was too violent for kids, to which Dahl argued that children like the gruesome parts of his books and enjoy it for the fantasy that it is. He said later, "My nastiness is never gratuitous. It's retribution. Beastly people must be punished."[111] One criticism that Dahl agreed with was the widespread belief that it was wrong to depict the Oompa-Loompas as black pygmies deported from Africa. Dahl later revised the book so that the Oompa-Loompas had long wavy hair and came from an imaginary island called Loompaland.

By the time the book was first published in America, Dahl had another daughter, named Ophelia, and his wife was soon pregnant again. Tragedy, however, wasn't far behind. During the early stage of her pregnancy, Pat suffered a series of three strokes, which left her unable to speak and partially paralyzed. Dahl put all of his effort into helping Pat recover, but it was slow and frustrating for both of them. Fortunately, their baby, named Lucy, was born perfectly healthy.

To help their financial situation, Dahl began writing screenplays. He wrote a James Bond movie called *You Only Live Twice*, followed by *Chitty Chitty Bang Bang*, and in 1970 he wrote the movie version of *Charlie and the Chocolate Factory*. The movie became a huge hit, and the sales of Dahl's books doubled. Gradually Pat was able to work again and their life settled down into a pleasant routine.

A Writer Writes

Dahl became a very dedicated writer of children's books. He kept a strict daily writing schedule and always used the same type of pencil. He jotted down notes in his ever-present red notebook, claiming that every one of his books got its start as a word or phrase from that notebook. *Charlie and the Chocolate Factory* came out of a note that read, "What about a chocolate factory that makes marvelous and fantastic things—with a crazy man running it?"[112] Although Dahl loved writing books, he didn't think it was easy, and he often argued with his publishers, editors, and accountants.

The life of a writer is absolute hell compared with the life of a businessman. The writer has to force himself to work. He has to make his own hours and if he doesn't go to his desk at all there is nobody to scold him. If he is a writer of fiction he lives in a world of fear. Each new day demands new ideas and he can never be sure whether he is going to come up with them or not.[113]

Dahl claimed that after two hours of writing fiction he was drained and had to take a break (which usually meant a glass of scotch). In the last two decades of his life he wrote nearly twenty best-selling children's books (including *Charlie and the Great Glass Elevator; The BFG*, which instantly became one of his most popular books; *The Witches;* and *Matilda*), six of which were made into successful movies. Many of his books were illustrated by the award-winning artist Quentin Blake, a collaboration that Dahl treasured. Between 1980 and 1990, over 11 million of Dahl's books were sold in paperback in Britain alone, which was much more than the total number of children born there during that time. In fact, it was figured that by 1990 one out of three British children bought or was given a book written by Dahl each year.

In his last two decades of life, Dahl wrote almost twenty award-winning novels, including Matilda *and* The BFG.

After thirty years of marriage, Dahl and Pat divorced in 1983, and at sixty-six years old, Dahl married Felicity Crosland, a considerably younger woman. He had hoped to be knighted by the queen, but he had to settle for three Edgar Allan Poe Awards for his short stories and one Whitbread Award for *The Witches*. After battling with his health for years, he succumbed to leukemia on November 23, 1990. Much of his money went into forming the Roald Dahl Foundation, which gives grants to worthwhile causes. Of her father, Lucy Dahl recalls,

> It was always such a treat to have dinner with him or be at the dining-room table when he was there. He was always pushing people to be at their best and there was lots of laughter and delicious food. He was definitely the king of our family and we all adored him.[114]

Today children from all over the world visit Dahl's grave and leave little treasures behind, proving that they, too, still adore him.

CHAPTER 7

Maurice Sendak

If I have an unusual gift, it is not that I draw particularly better or write particularly better than other people—I've never fooled myself of that. Rather, it's that I remember things other people don't recall: the sounds and feelings and images—the emotional quality of particular moments in childhood.[115]

It is my involvement with this inescapable fact of childhood—the awful vulnerability of children and their struggle to make themselves King of all Wild Things—that gives my work whatever truth and passion it may have.[116]

—Maurice Sendak

As the creator of more than eighty books for children, Maurice Sendak is considered by one prominent literary scholar to be "one of the principal mythologists of modern childhood. His works weave the intensely felt experiences of his own childhood and his continuing contact with its dynamic forces into the textures of a living mythology."[117] Sendak is known around the world for portraying childhood in an honest way through the use of fantasy. He doesn't sugarcoat the experiences and longings of children; rather, he allows his readers to recognize themselves through the behavior, emotions, fears, and sensuality of his characters. He says, "My books are written . . . for children who are never satisfied with condescending material, who understand real emotion and real feeling . . . and who are not afraid of knowing emotional truth."[118] Dubbed "The Picasso of Children's Books," Sendak is credited with redefining the kind of books that are appealing to, and appropriate for, the youngest reader. His beautifully rendered illustrations and potentially frightening storylines created a virtual revolution in picture books and have made him one of the most loved authors/illustrators in America.

First-Generation American

Maurice Sendak was born on June 10, 1928, in Brooklyn, New York. His brother, Jack, was five years older than him, and his sister, Natalie, was ten years older. His parents, Philip and Sarah, were both from Poland, and they often filled their children's heads with stories of the old country. Often sick as a child, Sendak spent a good deal of his childhood watching other kids run around the neighborhood. When he was healthy, he was permitted to join them. He recalls, "You were never allowed to cross the street, walk in the gutter, or come upstairs except at mealtime or to go to the bathroom or to stop profuse bleeding. Food and other necessaries were dropped out the window, and street fights were screechingly arbitrated by mamas in adjacent windows."[119]

His family was close, and as the youngest child, Sendak was well loved and protected. But he was very aware of fear. Though his father was always able to provide for the family, they only had the bare essentials. When World War II began, a sense of fear and dread permeated the household, and the worst was realized when, on the morning of Sendak's bar mitzvah, they learned that their relatives in Poland had been killed. When Sendak recalls the things that frightened him as a child besides the war, he lists "the vacuum cleaner, my sister, a very few ordinary horrors from movies, books, the radio, the Lindbergh baby kidnapping, and, finally, school, for which I had a desperate loathing."[120] A shy boy, Sendak hated school, believing that its strict rules and crowded classrooms robbed children of their individuality.

Since Sendak was so often bedridden, he developed an early love for books. He treasured the feel of books as much as their content. He loved how a book with a fine cover felt and how the pages smelled. When his sister presented him with his own copy of *The Prince and the Pauper,* he couldn't help but try to bite its shiny, laminated cover. Reading it would come later. He spent his bedridden years reading books like *A Child's Garden of Verses, Babar the Elephant, The Back of the North Wind* by George MacDonald, and *Grimms' Fairy Tales.* Not willing to be outdone by his older siblings, Sendak also read books intended for older children like *Tom Sawyer, Huckleberry Finn,* and anything by Herman Melville. When he wasn't reading, he was drawing in his notebooks, mostly scenes from the neighborhood. He also loved the early, spunky version of Mickey Mouse and the spirit of adventure he demonstrated. The artist inside him recognized something else special about Mickey: "A good deal of my pleasure in Mickey had to do with his bizarre proportions: the great rounded head extended still farther by those black saucer ears, the black trunk fitting snugly into ballooning red shorts, the tiny legs stuffed into delicious doughy yellow shoes. The giant white gloves, yellow buttons, pie-cut eyes, and bewitching grin were the delectable finishing touches."[121] This early edition of Mickey inspired Sendak's own artistic vision, and he named the main character of his favorite book (*In the Night Kitchen*) after him.

Beginnings

Sendak's talent as an artist was recognized at an early age. While still in high school he landed a job filling in the backgrounds for the syndicated *Mutt and Jeff* cartoon. He also did the illustrations for a science textbook called *Atomics for the Millions*. After graduation he worked as a display dresser for the toy store FAO Schwartz in New York City and took night classes at the Art Students League. He lived at home in Brooklyn and filled sketchbooks with drawings and overheard conversations of the neighborhood children. While at FAO Schwartz he gravitated often to the children's book section, where he fell in love with the work of famous illustrators like Randolph Caldecott. He saw how a great picture book was a combination of rhythm and structure, and he knew that he wanted to be a part of that world. The head of the children's book department introduced him to the esteemed editor at Harper and Brothers publishing, Ursula Nordstrom, who immediately loved his work. She hired him to illustrate a book called *The Wonderful Farm* by Marcel Ayme. Sendak considered Nordstrom to be his best friend and the guardian angel of his career. In 1952, she hired him to illustrate a book with well-known children's writer Ruth Krauss. The resulting collaboration, *A Hole Is to Dig,* propelled Sendak into the limelight.

Living in Greenwich Village with his beloved dog, Jennie, Sendak kept very busy illustrating other people's books, receiving great reviews. The *Little Bear* series, written by Else Holmelund Minarik, allowed Sendak to hone his skills as an artist, and the charm and grace of his illustrations endeared him to his contemporaries and his young audience. It wasn't until 1956 that he illustrated a book he had also written, *Kenny's Window.* This endeavor allowed Sendak to explore the themes that would reappear in his books throughout his career—the struggle of every child to "integrate his fantasies and fears with real-life experience; to have faith in his dreams and thereby gain mastery over the circumstances of his life. . . . [Sendak] permits his hero to be angry, unjust, and even cruel at times—just like children in the real world."[122]

In 1960, Sendak put his old neighborhood sketchbook to good use when he published *The Sign on Rosie's Door*, starring one of the children he used to watch on his block named Rosie. Rosie "was a fierce child who impressed me with her ability to imagine herself into being anything she wanted to be, anywhere in or out of the world. She literally forced her fantasies on her more stolid, less driven friends, and the tremendous energy she put into these dream games probably activated my own creativity."[123] From this book came another set of four small books starring Rosie's friends called *The Nutshell Library*, which earned Sendak the American Library Association's Notable Book Award. Together these ventures would spawn the timeless animated television special *Really Rosie*, and an off-Broadway play with the same name.

By age thirty-four, Sendak had illustrated fifty books—seven of which he also wrote. It was time for something big, and when it arrived, it was in the form of some very big, very wild monsters.

Sendak at his home workshop in Greenwich Village, New York.

Let the Wild Rumpus Start

In 1963, Sendak published the first of what would be a trilogy of books exploring children's responses to strong emotions. *Where the Wild Things Are* is the story of a little boy named Max whose anger gets him sent to bed without supper. Dressed in his wolf pajamas, he embarks on a trip to the land of the Wild Things, who he quickly dominates before growing tired and returning home to find his still-hot supper waiting for him. The response to this book from children was very powerful. The *Library Journal* reported that a little girl who had never spoken and had withdrawn from the world around her spoke her first sentence after a teacher's aide read her the book. Her sentence was, "Can I have that book?"[124] The response from librarians, reviewers, and educators was also very swift. Some worried that the themes (and the monsters) in the book might scare children. This reaction surprised Sendak, who believes that children "continually cope with frustration as best as they can . . . fear and anxiety are an intrinsic part of their everyday lives. And it is through fantasy that children achieve catharsis. It is the best means they have for taming Wild Things."[125] He points out that through his adventure into a fantasy world, Max rids himself of his anger.

The book was groundbreaking in the world of children's literature. Sendak believes it was because "Before that, a children's

Maurice Sendak with a character model from his book Where the Wild Things Are.

book was supposed to be kept immaculate, in terms of sex, in terms of anger, in terms of death, in terms of anything to do with life . . . but of course that's all kids ever want to know about. Which is why the Grimms are so popular."[126]

In 1964 the book won the highest honor possible—the Caldecott Medal, presented annually by the American Library Association to the finest picture book of the preceding year. In his acceptance speech, Sendak said, "With *Where the Wild Things Are* I feel that I am at the end of a long apprenticeship. By that I mean all my previous work now seems to have been an elaborate preparation for it."[127] He later explained that the Wild Things themselves were based on overbearing relatives who came for dinner when he was a child. He remembers them smothering him, and when they said, "You look so good, we could eat you up," Sendak was afraid they meant it. After nearly four decades, the book is as popular as ever. "Little Max has done well for his father," says Sendak. "There are very few five-year-olds who support their fathers the way he does and God bless the little bugger."[128] Max brought more than financial success to Sendak; the book allowed him the flexibility to continue expressing himself with more unique, history-making projects.

The Method to His Madness

Sendak's routine has remained the same, whether working out of his Greenwich Village studio or his current home in woodsy Connecticut. A huge fan of Mozart, Sendak has always listened to classical music while drawing. Each book requires its own background accompaniment. He explains that "Sketching to music is a marvelous stimulant to my imagination, and often a piece of music will give me the needed clue to the look and color of a picture."[129] It's a different story when he's working on the text, however. Then he needs absolute quiet. For Sendak, the words come first, and since it is more difficult for him to write than to draw, he gets more satisfaction out of the writing. "I don't think in pictures at all," he says. "Sometimes after I've written something I find that there are things in my story that I don't draw well . . . but I've written it and I'm stuck with it."[130]

For Sendak, the writing process is a cleansing process as well as a creative one. By delving into his memories and childhood fears and handing them over to his characters, Sendak rids himself of his ghosts by writing them out of his life. As for his artwork, he refuses to settle on any one style, feeling that he would get trapped and bored. His style changes considerably from book to book, depending on what he feels the story demands. In his studio, filled with familiar and strange objects and artifacts, books, and rare Mickey Mouse toys, Sendak becomes completely immersed in his current project. Sometimes he is so consumed that the story seeps into his dreams, and he will go for months without socializing with other people. When illustrating the work of other writers he often chooses stories where his illustrations can bring out something new. Success came easily to Sendak, and he was very happy with his chosen career. It wasn't until he suffered a severe heart attack in 1967 that he realized he wasn't invincible.

Facing Mortality

Sendak was only thirty-eight years old, at a speaking engagement in England, when he wound up in the hospital, shocked at his close call with death. "I was amazed. I couldn't believe it was happening—that my mission could be cut short like that. I felt as though a bargain had been broken, that so long as I kept working and honestly recalling my childhood, I had been granted some sort of immunity."[131] He was forced to stay in England for many weeks until he recovered. Discharged on his thirty-ninth birthday, Sendak returned to America to care for his beloved dog, Jennie, who had been diagnosed with cancer. To deal with his grief, he wrote *Higglety Pigglety Pop!* which was published a few weeks after his dog had been put to sleep. While in mourning for Jennie, Sendak also had to deal with his mother's battle with cancer. When she died a year later, he was devastated. For two years he worked on a project that would "say goodbye to New York and say goodbye to my parents, and tell a bit about the narrow squeak I had just been through."[132] When *In the Night Kitchen* was finally published in 1970, it made quite a stir in the children's book world, and propelled Sendak into the record books as the first American to win the world-renowned Hans Christian Andersen Medal for illustration.

Controversy and Kudos

At the same time that *In the Night Kitchen* won Sendak a Caldecott honor citation (the runner-up to the medal itself, one of seven he was to earn over the next three decades), it lost him a few friends among librarians and teachers. Some educators deemed the book offensive because the main character—a little boy named Mickey—was pictured naked throughout a good deal of the book. Sendak was surprised, once again, to be the object of controversy and censorship. He argued that the critics were missing the point, that the book simply celebrated the sensory world of the child's imagination. It was inspired by an advertisement from his childhood that boasted, "We Bake While You Sleep." Sendak said that as a child it seemed that "everything good was done while I was sleeping—everything! Kids feel like they're put to bed and then [the adults] have fun. *In the Night Kitchen* became a vendetta to see just what goes on . . . it was a fantasy of what I wished to do my whole childhood."[133] No matter how Sendak argued for his book, or how many awards it won, or how much kids loved it, some librarians insisted on drawing shorts on little Mickey before putting it on their shelves.

In 1981, Sendak published the final book in his "facing childhood emotions" trilogy, called *Outside over There*. It is about a little girl who is entrusted with the care of her baby sister and then has to rescue the baby when it is stolen by goblins. The book was Sendak's way of showing the reality of sibling relationships. Of his own sister, he said, "Today my sister is a good, loving woman who lives in New Jersey. But at nine, she was a raving psychopath who was out to kill me."[134] The book, which Sendak considers his finest, was a very personal endeavor—one that he claims finally brought him inner peace.

Let the Wild Rumpus Continue

In 1988, Sendak made publishing history when the first printing of his book based on a Grimm fairy tale, *Dear Mili*, numbered 250,000 copies. This was by far the largest number for a first print run of a children's book. Now seventy-one, Sendak shows no signs of slowing down. He has expanded his artistic endeavors to include designing sets and costumes for operas and ballets, and he hopes that the children's theater company he cofounded with author Arthur Yorinks in 1990 (called the Night Kitchen) continues to thrive.

Where the Wild Things Are has been translated into sixteen languages since its publication in 1963, and Sendak has adapted it into plays, operas, and musicals. The monsters have been turned into cuddly stuffed animals and enormous helium balloons for the Macy's Thanksgiving Day Parade; they have also been used in advertising and literacy campaigns. In 1999, the Metreon, a huge entertainment center, opened in San Francisco. The top level is modeled on Sendak's books. The family-style restaurant is called In the Night Kitchen, and a playground based on *Where the Wild Things Are* allows kids to finally reach the land of the Wild Things.

A stage performance of Where the Wild Things Are.

Throughout his career Sendak has illustrated works by some of the finest writers in the world, including Randall Jarrell, Herman Melville, E. T. A. Hoffman, William Blake, Robert Graves, the Grimm brothers, George MacDonald, and Isaac Bashevis Singer. His touch is unmistakable and always raises the material to a new level. His most recent book, 1999's *Swine Lake,* was a collaboration with his best friend, the late author/illustrator of the George and Martha books, James Marshall. Sendak's most recent honors have been the prestigious Laura Ingalls Wilder Award and the 1998 Jewish Cultural Achievement Award. He is grateful for the recognition by the publishing industry, but what matters most to him are the children who read his books. He claims he can barely hold back the tears when "Every year parents who were little people when I wrote *[Where the Wild Things Are]* present their children to me. And here are these new human beings with their eyes beaming, and they are again in wolf suits."[135]

CHAPTER 8

Judy Blume

Sometimes reading books that deal with other kids who feel the same things they do, it makes them feel less alone. I have a wonderful, intimate relationship with kids. They feel that they know me and that I know them. I have a capacity for total recall. I have this gift, this memory, so it's easy to project myself back to certain stages in my life. And I write about what I know is true of kids going through those same stages.[136]

—Judy Blume

With book sales of over 65 million copies in twenty languages, Judy Blume is the most popular children's and young adult novelist of her generation. As one educator pointed out, "There is, indeed, scarcely a literate girl of novel-reading age who has not read one or more Blume books."[137] Blume's audience isn't only female. A male professor from Yale University noted, "When I got to college, there was no author except Shakespeare whom more of my peers had read."[138] From the very start, Blume used her insight into the adolescent mind to herald a new type of book for young people—realistic fiction. One scholar explains,

> She writes as though filming the landscape of childhood from the eye level of a child. She focuses on nearby objects and immediate events with a child's intense gaze, picking out the details that evoke instant recognition. We have the feeling we are reading a secret diary. . . . The effect is a mesmerizing intimacy, which convinces Judy's readers that she writes the whole truth about what kids think and feel.[139]

In her effort to present the concerns of young people truthfully, Blume broke through boundaries previously considered taboo.

While children around the world embraced her for her willingness to tackle difficult issues like sexuality, divorce, peer cruelty, and sibling rivalry, some parents and librarians felt differently. Blume now has the unique position of being at the same time the most widely read author for young people in the world and the most banned.

Growing Up in Suburbia

Judy Blume was born Judy Sussman on February 12, 1938, in Elizabeth, New Jersey. Her father, Rudolph, was a dentist, and her mother, Esther, took care of Judy and her older brother, David. Every room of their house was filled with books, and Judy's mother was always reading. A shy, sensitive girl, Judy used to go with her mother to the library. It was there that she discovered her favorite book, *Madeline* by Ludwig Bemelmans, and began her lifelong love of books. When she got a little older she devoured the *Betsy-Tacy* series, the *Nancy Drew* series, and the Oz books by L. Frank Baum.

Judy would pretend to be a character from whatever book she was currently reading. She dreamed of becoming a movie star one day and a spy the next. Her father encouraged her by letting her know she could be anything she wanted to be, even though in that era girls didn't have many career opportunities. Judy and her father were very close, and she was always frightened that he would die young, since both of his brothers died at age forty-two. She made up elaborate prayer rituals to keep him safe, and when he finally turned forty-three, she was overcome with joy.

When she was in third grade, her brother became ill and needed to be in warm weather to get better. The family decided to move to Florida for the year, but Judy's father had to stay in New Jersey to work. At first Judy hated Miami Beach, but she soon made close friends, and she loved being able to play outdoors even in the winter. The move was an important stage in Judy's life because she learned that she was likable enough to make new friends easily and adventurous enough to try new things.

Back home in New Jersey, her childhood was once again filled with activities. She took dance, piano, and drawing lessons; roller-skated; read books; played with her friends; and went to summer camp. She was very popular and had a busy social life. It wasn't until she became a teenager that she began questioning things and realized nobody was able to provide the answers. She began to feel very alone, even surrounded by her many friends.

Teen Angst

At twelve years old, Blume says, "I kind of lost myself. I think of my life up to age eleven or twelve as one kind of life, and then a different kind of life took over. The pressure to conform kicked in and I was completely concerned with being accepted, and how I looked, and my clothes, and all kinds of stupid junk."[140] She formed a secret club with a group of girlfriends called the Pre-Teen Kittens. Their main concerns were which boys they liked and who would get their menstrual period first—important aspects of a preadolescent girl's life. Blume says, "I think I write about sexuality [now] because it was uppermost in my mind when I was a kid: the need to know, and not knowing how to find out . . . questions about what I was feeling, and how my body could feel, I *never* asked my parents."[141]

Judy Blume, author of dozens of books written specifically for struggling adolescents.

During this time Judy began to pull away from her family, even from her father. She acted the role of the "good girl," always wanting her parents to be proud of her. She felt like it was her responsibility to pretend that everything was great even though inside she was confused about a lot of things. She wanted to talk to her mother about more serious topics than dances and dresses, but she didn't know how. At fifteen she went away to a new sleep-away camp, where, unlike at her last camp, she didn't make friends. The lowest point of her summer was when she received a call from her parents telling her that her beloved grandmother had died. Even though her family had seen a lot of death, nobody had talked to Judy about what it felt like to lose someone you love. She suffered her loss deeply, and she suffered it alone.

When she got to high school she threw herself into even more activities than she had in the past. She was very social with her friends, sang in the chorus, worked for the newspaper, and acted in school plays. Battin High was a large, all-girls school in Elizabeth. Even though Judy and her friends complained about the lack of boys at the time, she now believes it gave the girls more opportunities to express themselves and to take on bigger roles in school.

Judy enjoyed learning different things and always worked hard. She was accepted at Boston University and expected to be there for the whole four years. She barely lasted a week.

Clipping Her Wings

Even before her parents dropped her off at Boston University, Judy had been suffering from a terrible headache. Assuming it was just nerves, she didn't tell anyone about it. After a few days at school, however, she collapsed and had to be flown back to New Jersey. She was embarrassed because it turned out she had mononucleosis, which was known as "the kissing disease." She had to stay in bed for over a month, and by the time she was well enough to return to school, she decided to attend nearby New York University instead. During this time her parents moved to Westfield, New Jersey, a few towns away from where Judy grew up. Over Christmas vacation her sophomore year, Judy was invited to a party in her new neighborhood, where she met a young lawyer named John Blume. A year later he asked her to marry him, and she said yes.

A few days before the wedding in August 1959, the family went to pick up Judy's brother, David, at the airport. David announced that his wife was pregnant, and everybody was thrilled, especially Judy and David's father, who felt blessed that such exciting things were happening in his children's lives. An hour later, Judy watched in anguish as her father died of a sudden heart attack. She had lost the most important man in her life and everything was about to change. She was only twenty-one years old.

In 1961, Blume earned her bachelor's degree in education. But her plan of teaching second grade would have to wait, because she was pregnant. Her daughter Randy was born that same year and was joined two years later by a son named Larry. Now living in a large house in suburban Scotch Plains, New Jersey, Blume settled into life as a homemaker. She was happy for a few years, until she realized something was missing. She felt like her creative fire was dying out, and when her children started nursery school she decided to do something about it.

Trial and Error

Blume first tried songwriting, but she soon gave that up in favor of making colorful, personalized felt banners for kids' bedrooms. She got a few orders from stores, but after a year of cutting and pasting in her basement, she became allergic to the glue and had to stop. Then it occurred to her that maybe she could write the kinds of books she was reading to her young children. With Dr. Seuss as her role model, she tried writing rhyming picture books. She sent them out to publishing companies and was so devastated by her first rejection that she closed herself in her closet and wept.

In order to learn more about writing, Blume signed up for a night course at her alma mater, NYU. The class, taught by writer Lee Wyndham, was called "Writing for Children and Teenagers." She loved it so much, she took it twice. Her teacher was very supportive, and two and a half years after she got her first rejection slip, Blume began getting acceptance letters instead. Two of her short stories for young children were published in magazines, and in 1969, Reilly and Lee Publishers accepted a short picture book, *The One in the Middle Is the Green Kangaroo*. Jumping around the house, Blume was absolutely ecstatic when she got the call about the book publication. She said later, "I don't think anything is as exciting as that first acceptance."[142] Her husband, John, was pleased that she was succeeding, but he didn't really understand why it was so important to her. Her community thought it was a quaint hobby, and an article about her was published with the headline "Mom Keeps Busy Writing Books for Little Children." As Blume says, "Feminism came late to suburbia. I lived on a street with thirty houses and not one woman worked. I didn't fit in. I knew I didn't fit in. And maybe that's when I stopped trying so hard."[143]

She didn't stop trying to get published, however. Blume learned of a new publishing house called Bradbury Press that was looking for realistic fiction. She knew she wanted to write about real kids going through real experiences feeling real emotions. Dick Jackson, a young editor at Bradbury, invited her to come to the office. Although she was terrified at meeting a real editor face-to-face, Jackson made her feel at ease. She showed him a book she had written about a black family who moves into a white neighborhood. He

Blume's first stories were published in 1969.

gave her suggestions on making it better, and she devoted all her time to revising it. The book, *Iggie's House,* was published by Bradbury in 1970. Even though some critics called it "overly simplistic" and Blume agreed it could have been tighter, it was her first novel and she was proud of it. Before the novel even came out Blume already had the idea for her next book, for slightly older children. It would be the story of a twelve-year-old girl on the brink of growing up. It would be an honest, intimate look at what went on inside the girl's head. *Are You There God? It's Me, Margaret* would not only change Blume's life forever, it would transform the entire landscape of children's literature.

Are You There God? It's Me, Margaret.

"I'd published two books and several short stories before *Margaret,*" Blume said, "but I hadn't found my voice yet. I hadn't written from deep inside. With *Margaret* I found my voice and my audience."[144] Writing straight from her heart and her memory of being a twelve-year-old girl, Blume completed *Are You There God? It's Me, Margaret* in only six weeks. When it was published in late 1970, it immediately received praise. The *New York Times* called it, "A warm, funny and loving book, one that captures the essence of adolescence,"[145] and it named it one of the outstanding children's books of the year. *Publisher's Weekly* stated that, with "sensitivity and humor," Blume captured "the joys, fears and uncertainty that surround a young girl approaching adolescence."[146]

Blume's intended audience loved the book as well. Young girls felt like she knew exactly what they were thinking, and they identified with Margaret's concerns about becoming a woman. As a result, they started writing Blume letters, confiding their problems and secrets. Blume realized that, just as she had been twenty years earlier, this new generation was hungry for books that would show them they weren't alone. As one reviewer noted, by writing in the first person as though Margaret was the one presenting the story, Blume "succeeds in establishing intimacy and identification between character and audience. All her books read like diaries or journals and the reader is drawn in by the narrator's self-revelations."[147]

Preteens quickly made the book a best-seller, but the backlash was about to begin. Never before had an author for young people presented a girl stuffing her bra or worrying about getting her first menstrual period. The book also deals with Margaret's confusion about religion and the fear and excitement of her first kiss. When Judy gave copies of the book to her children's school, the administrators refused to put them on the library shelves because the book dealt with such sensitive topics. Other schools across the country similarly banned the book from their libraries, sometimes bowing to pressure from concerned parents. This type of censorship surprised and angered Blume, who had never set out to write anything controversial. She argued that "it's sad that puberty should be an issue of controversy, since it's going to happen to everybody, whether their parents like it or not."[148] The censorship of *Are You There God? It's Me, Margaret* was only the beginning, however, because Judy Blume had a lot more to say.

Most Popular, Most Banned

It never occurred to Blume to shy away from potentially sensitive or controversial subjects. The very next year she published *Then Again, Maybe I Won't*, which she considered to be the companion to *Are You There God? It's Me, Margaret*. Through the character of thirteen-year-old Tony Miglione, young boys were now discovering that their problems were normal too. Together, the two books gave preteens invaluable insight into the opposite sex. As before, reviewers praised the new book for its groundbreaking portrayal of a young boy on the verge of adolescence, and censors once again banned it.

Blume believes that "censorship grows out of fear . . . book banning satisfies parents' need to feel in control of their children's lives. This fear is often disguised as moral outrage. They want to believe that if their children don't read about it, their children won't know about it, and if they don't know about it, it won't happen."[149] Blume continued to cause a stir with *Deenie, Blubber*, and *Forever*. *Forever* was intended to be for older readers than her previous books (young adults instead of preteens). Instead, it was quickly snatched up by sixth and seventh graders who underlined the racy passages and passed the book around their classes. Blume said she hoped kids wouldn't read the book until they thought they were emotionally ready for it and that they would discuss it afterward with their parents. Many school libraries refused to circulate the book, and public libraries often shelved it in the adult department. Twenty-one years after it was published, *Forever* earned Blume her only major award from the young adult division of the American Library Association. The Margaret A. Edwards Award honors one author each year for his or her outstanding contribution to young adult literature. As one educator wrote, "In 1975, when the heroine of *Forever* decided to go on the pill, the book was daring. Now it is quaint. But it is precisely that quaintness that allows us to recognize Judy Blume

Selling over 65 million books worldwide, Judy Blume has become one of the most prolific children's authors of our time.

properly. In this age of [children's books like] *Heather Has Two Mommies,* we clearly live after the flood. We might pause to thank the author who opened the gates."[150] This award did just that.

Not every book Blume wrote was controversial. Her publisher calls *Tales of a Fourth Grade Nothing, Otherwise Known as Sheila the Great,* and the *Fudge* series, Judy's "merry books." Kids love these titles just as much as the others, and in fact *Tales* has sold the most copies, with *Margaret* a close second. *Starring Sally J. Freedman as Herself,* published in 1977, is closest to Blume's heart because it is the most autobiographical. Facing criticism about how she portrayed her main character's feelings about religion, Blume explained it was based on her own Jewish background: "Dressing up and going to Temple on the High Holy Days was very much a social thing. I never felt God in a synagogue, but I surely felt him when I was alone."[151] It was easy for Blume to escape into the memories of her stable, loving childhood and to turn them into books that kids loved to read. It was harder for her to face that her adult life had suddenly become anything *but* stable.

Hiding Behind Her Typewriter

Working out of her house forced Blume to become disciplined, so she developed a very organized writing process. She worked seven days a week, even if just a little each day. She kept notes in a notebook and on any available scrap of paper or tissue. Before writing each book, she made sure she knew her characters very well and knew where the story was heading. She enjoyed the process of rewriting, so she completed four or five drafts of each book, with intense revision near the end, before she considered it ready for publication. After writing ten books in six years, Blume considered quitting. She was feeling lonely and slowly faced the fact that she was no longer happy in her marriage.

After sixteen years together, Judy and John Blume divorced in 1975. Confused and on the rebound, Judy married a man she hardly knew and moved her children to Santa Fe, New Mexico. It didn't take her long to realize she had made a mistake, and three years later she divorced again. She explains that she remarried so quickly because "I didn't know how to be unmarried. I cried every day. Anyone who thinks my life was cupcakes all the way is wrong. Work really saved me. I've always been able to write, even when everything else was falling apart."[152]

On her own for the next eight years, Blume split her time between Santa Fe and New York City. In 1987, she married nonfiction writer George Cooper. Very happy together, they now split their time between Key West, Florida; Martha's Vineyard, Massachusetts; and New York City. But Blume isn't slowing down.

Giving Something Back

One thing that Blume learned from all the letters she has received (and continues to receive) from kids and teenagers is that there needs to be stronger communication between children and their parents. In 1981, she founded the KIDS Fund, which gives grants to nonprofit organizations that focus on projects to foster intergenerational communication. The royalties from 1986's *Letters to Judy: What Your Kids Wish They Could Tell You*, along with royalties from some of Blume's other projects, are donated to the fund. This generosity earned her the Carl Sandburg Freedom to Read Award in 1984 and the American Civil Liberties Union Award in 1986.

Blume is also an active spokesperson for the National Coalition Against Censorship, arguing that "the way to instill values in children is to talk about difficult issues and bring them out in the open, not to restrict their access to books that may help them deal with their problems and concerns."[153] She feels that society can't expect kids to cope with life as an adult if they aren't encouraged to face reality when they are young. And she won't stop fighting against censorship as long as groups keep publishing things like the Religious Right Movement's pamphlet "How to Rid Your School Library of Judy Blume Books."

Over her thirty-year career of writing children's books (and three for adults), Blume has won more than ninety awards. Her books have been adapted into animated television shows and live-action television movies. Publishers continue to update and modernize her book covers, and she still receives over a thousand letters a month from her readers. Even though she is now a grandmother, she says that inside she is "always twelve, forever twelve. That's me, yes. You can be a grandma and still be twelve inside . . . and I guess those of us who hang on to the really early ages are the ones who feel most comfortable writing about it."[154] This gift of transporting herself back into the shoes of a twelve-year-old helps explain why the president of the Assembly on Literature for Adolescents once proclaimed, "There probably hasn't been any other writer in history who is as popular."[155]

NOTES

Introduction

1. Quoted inThomas Fensch, ed., *Of Sneetches and Whos and the Good Dr. Seuss: Essays on the Writings and Life of Theodor Geisel.* Jefferson, NC: McFarland, 1997.

2. Anita Silvey, ed., *Children's Books and Their Creators.* Boston: Houghton Mifflin, 1995.

3. Jeremy Treglown, *Roald Dahl: A Biography.* New York: Farrar, Straus, Giroux, 1994.

4. Quoted in Charlotte Cory, "Life Story: The Woman Who Drew Narnia," *Daily Telegraph,* September 19, 1998.

5. Anita Silvey, "The Problem with Trends," *Horn Book Magazine,* September/October 1995.

Chapter 1: The History and Importance of Writing Books for Children

6. E. L. Konigsburg, *TalkTalk: A Children's Book Author Speaks to Grown-Ups.* New York: Atheneum, 1995.

7. C. S. Lewis, *An Experiment in Criticism.* Cambridge, England: Cambridge University Press, 1961.

8. Quoted in Alison Lurie, *Don't Tell the Grown-Ups: Subversive Children's Literature.* Boston: Little, Brown, 1990.

9. Lurie, *Don't Tell the Grown-Ups.*

10. Lurie, *Don't Tell the Grown-Ups.*

Chapter 2: A. A. Milne

11. A. A. Milne, *By Way of Introduction.* London: Methuen, 1929.

12. *Life,* "The World of Pooh Lives On," February 1956.

13. Quoted in Ann Thwaite, *A. A. Milne: The Man Behind Winnie-the-Pooh.* New York: Random House, 1990.

14. John Rowe Townsend, *Twentieth Century Children's Literature.* Ed. Tracy Chevalier. Chicago: St. James Press, 1989.

15. A. A. Milne, *Autobiography.* New York: Dutton, 1939.

16. Milne, *Autobiography.*

17. Milne, *Autobiography.*

18. Milne, *Autobiography.*

19. Milne, *Autobiography.*

20. Milne, *Autobiography.*

21. A. A. Milne, *When We Were Very Young.* New York: Dutton, 1924.

22. Quoted in Ann Thwaite, *The Brilliant Career of Winnie-the-Pooh.* New York: Dutton's Children's Books, 1994.

23. Quoted in Thwaite, *The Brilliant Career of Winnie-the-Pooh.*

24. Milne, *Autobiography.*

25. Milne, *Autobiography.*

26. Quoted in Thwaite, *The Brilliant Career of Winnie-the-Pooh.*

27. Lurie, *Don't Tell the Grown-Ups.*

28. Quoted in Thwaite, *A. A. Milne.*

29. A. A. Milne, *The House at Pooh Corner.* New York: Dutton, 1928.

30. Christopher Milne, *The Enchanted Places.* New York: Dutton, 1975.

31. Milne, *By Way of Introduction.*

32. Quoted in Thwaite, *The Brillliant Career of Winnie the Pooh.*

33. Quoted in Thwaite, *A. A. Milne.*

34. Paula T. Connolly, *Winnie-the-Pooh and The House at Pooh Corner: Recovering Arcadia.* New York: Twayne, 1995.

35. Marcus Crouch, *Treasure Seekers and Borrowers: Children's Books in Britain.* London: Library Association, 1962.

36. Quoted in Thwaite, *The Brilliant Career of Winnie-the-Pooh.*

Chapter 3: C. S. Lewis

37. C. S. Lewis, *On Stories and Other Essays on Literature.* Ed. Walter Hooper. New York: Harcourt Brace Jovanovich, 1982.

38. C. S. Lewis, *Surprised by Joy: The Shape of My Early Life.* London: Geoffrey Bles, 1955.

39. Lewis, *Surprised by Joy.*

40. Lewis, *Surprised by Joy.*

41. Lewis, *Surprised by Joy.*

42. Lewis, *Surprised by Joy.*

43. Lewis, *Surprised by Joy.*

44. W. H. Lewis, *Letters of C. S. Lewis.* New York: Harcourt, Brace & World, 1966.

45. Lewis, *Letters of C. S. Lewis.*

46. Lewis, *Letters of C. S. Lewis.*

47. Lewis, *Surprised by Joy.*

48. Lewis, *On Stories and Other Essays on Literature.*

49. Quoted in James T. Como, ed., *C. S. Lewis at the Breakfast Table and Other Reminiscences.* New York: Macmillan, 1979.

50. Silvey, *Children's Books and Their Creators.*

51. Phoebe Pettingell, "Writers and Writing: C. S. Lewis' Romantic Egoism," *New Leader,* March 19, 1990.

52. Quoted in Brian Sibley, *The Land of Narnia: Brian Sibley Explores the World of C. S. Lewis.* New York: Harper and Row, 1989.

53. Quoted in Sibley, *The Land of Narnia.*

54. Lewis, *Letters of C. S. Lewis.*

55. Lewis, *Letters of C. S. Lewis.*

56. Quoted in Como, *C. S. Lewis at the Breakfast Table and Other Reminiscences.*

57. Quoted in Jay Copp, "A Touch of Narnia in Illinois," *Christian Science Monitor,* March 23, 1999.

58. Copp, "A Touch of Narnia in Illinois."

Chapter 4: E. B. White

59. E. B. White, "On Writing for Children," *Paris Review* 48, Fall 1969.

60. Roger Angell, "E. B. White," *New Yorker,* October 14, 1985.

61. Dorothy Lobrano Guth, ed. and compiler, *Letters of E. B. White.* New York: Harper, 1976.

62. Guth, *Letters of E. B. White.*

63. Guth, *Letters of E. B. White.*

64. Quoted in Beverly Gherman, *E. B. White: Some Writer!* New York: Atheneum, 1992.

65. E. B. White, *One Man's Meat: A New and Enlarged Edition.* New York: Harper & Brothers, 1944.

66. David R. Collins, *To the Point: A Story About E. B. White.* Minneapolis: CarolRhoda Books, 1989.

67. E. B. White, "A Strategem for Retirement," *Holiday,* March 1956.

68. E. B. White, *The Points of My Compass: Essays*. New York: Harper, 1962.

69. E. B. White, *Essays of E. B. White*. New York: Harper and Row, 1977.

70. Quoted in Janice Tingum, *E. B. White: The Elements of a Writer*. Minneapolis: Lerner, 1995.

71. Quoted in *New York Times*, "The Librarian Said It Was Bad for Children," March 6, 1966.

72. E. B. White, *Second Tree from the Corner*. New York: Harper, 1954.

73. Guth, *Letters of E. B. White*.

74. Bennett Cerf, *Saturday Review*, Jan. 3, 1953.

75. Quoted in Peter Neumeyer, *Annotated Charlotte's Web*. New York: HarperCollins, 1994.

76. Neumeyer, *Annotated Charlotte's Web*.

77. Guth, *Letters of E. B. White*.

78. Guth, *Letters of E. B. White*.

79. Quoted in Collins, *To the Point*.

80. Faith McNulty, "Children's Books for Christmas," *New Yorker*, November 25, 1991.

Chapter 5: Dr. Seuss

81. *In Search of Dr. Seuss* (videorecording). Atlanta: Turner Home Entertainment, 1994.

82. Quoted in Don Freeman, "Dr. Seuss at 72—Going Like 60," *Saturday Evening Post*, March 1977.

83. Quoted in James Stewart-Gordon, "Dr. Seuss: Fanciful State of Childhood," *Reader's Digest*, April 1972.

84. Quoted in Edward Connery Lathem, ed., "The Beginnings of Dr. Seuss: A Conversation with Theodor S. Geisel," *Dartmouth Alumni Magazine*, April 1976.

85. Quoted in Lathem, "The Beginnings of Dr. Seuss."

86. Quoted in Lathem, "The Beginnings of Dr. Seuss."

87. Quoted in Myra Kibler, *Dictionary of Literary Biography*, vol. 61, *American Writers for Children Since 1960*. Detroit, MI: Gale, 1987.

88. Quoted in Peter Bunzel, "The Wacky World of Dr. Seuss De-

lights the Child—and Adult—Readers of His Books," *Life,* April 6, 1959.

89. Dr. Seuss, *Horton Hatches the Egg.* New York: Random House, 1940.

90. Quoted in Bunzel, "The Wacky World of Dr. Seuss."

91. Quoted in Bunzel, "The Wacky World of Dr. Seuss."

92. Quoted in Arthur Gordon, "The Wonderful Wizard of Soledad Hill," *Women's Day,* September 1965.

93. Silvey, *Children's Books and Their Creators.*

94. Quoted in E. J. Kahn Jr., "Children's Friend," *New Yorker,* December 17, 1960.

95. Quoted in *Publisher's Weekly,* "Dr. Seuss Remembered," October 25, 1991.

96. Quoted in Freeman, "Dr. Seuss at 72—Going Like 60."

97. Quoted in Glenn Edward Sadler, "Maurice Sendak and Dr. Seuss: A Conversation," *Horn Book Magazine,* September/October 1989.

98. Quoted in Bunzel, "The Wacky World of Dr. Seuss."

99. Quoted in Ruth K. MacDonald, *Dr. Seuss.* Boston: Twayne, 1988.

100. Quoted in *Publisher's Weekly,* "Dr. Seuss Remembered."

Chapter 6: Roald Dahl

101. Quoted in Mark I. West, *Trust Your Children: Voices Against Censorship in Children's Literature.* New York: Neal-Schuman, 1988.

102. Quoted in *Writer,* August 1976.

103. Quoted in Karen Hershenson, "Kids Love Author's Black Humor, but Many Adults Have Their Doubts," *Contra Costa Times,* April 24, 1996.

104. Roald Dahl, *Boy.* New York: Farrar, Straus, Giroux, 1984.

105. Quoted in Roald Dahl, *The Wonderful Story of Henry Sugar and Six More.* New York: Knopf, 1977.

106. Dahl, *Boy.*

107. Mark I. West, *Roald Dahl.* New York: Twayne, 1992.

108. Quoted in Hershenson, "Kids Love Author's Black Humor."

109. Alfred A. Knopf, *Letter from July 5, 1960.* Archives of Alfred A. Knopf, Inc., Harry Ransom Humanities Research Center at the University of Texas at Austin.

110. Gerald Haigh, "For Non Squiffletrotters Only," *Times Educational Supplement,* November 19, 1982.

111. Quoted in Willa Petschek, "Roald Dahl at Home," *New York Times Book Review,* December 25, 1977.

112. Dahl, *The Wonderful World of Henry Sugar and Six More.*

113. Dahl, *Boy.*

114. Quoted in Hershenson, "Kids Love Author's Black Humor."

Chapter 7: Maurice Sendak

115. Quoted in John Banbury, "The Art of Maurice Sendak," November 1997. http://libserver.lib.flinders.edu.au/resources/collection/special/exhib/sendak.htm.

116. Maurice Sendak, *Caldecott & Co.: Notes on Books & Pictures.* New York: Farrar, Straus, Giroux, 1988.

117. John Cech, *Angels and Wild Things: The Archetypal Poetics of Maurice Sendak.* University Park: Pennsylvania State University Press, 1995.

118. Quoted in Silvey, *Children's Books and Their Creators.*

119. Sendak, *Caldecott & Co.*

120. Sendak, *Caldecott & Co.*

121. Sendak, *Caldecott & Co.*

122. Selma G. Lanes, *The Art of Maurice Sendak.* New York: Harry N. Abrams, 1980.

123. Sendak, *Caldecott & Co.*

124. Quoted in Marion Long, "Maurice Sendak: A Western Canon." http://homearts.com/depts/relat/sendakfl.htm.

125. Sendak, *Caldecott & Co.*

126. Quoted in Adam Langer, "Maurice Sendak: Dancing with Wolves," *Book Magazine,* May/June 1999.

127. Sendak, *Caldecott & Co.*

128. Quoted in Langer, "Maurice Sendak."

129. Sendak, *Caldecott & Co.*

130. Sendak, *Caldecott & Co.*

131. Quoted in Lanes, *The Art of Maurice Sendak.*

132. Quoted in Martha Shirk, "Gloomy Relatives Inspired Wild Things," *St. Louis Post-Dispatch,* December 4, 1989.

133. ICA Video, "Writing for Children." Northbrook, IL: Roland Collection, 1992.

134. ICA Video, "Writing for Children."

135. Quoted in Silvey, *Children's Books and Their Creators*.

Chapter 8: Judy Blume

136. Sybil Steinberg, "PW Interviews: Judy Blume," *Publisher's Weekly*, April 17, 1978.

137. Naomi Decter, "Judy Blume's Children," *Commentary*, March 1980.

138. Mark Oppenheimer, "Why Judy Blume Endures," *New York Times Book Review*, November 16, 1997.

139. Faith McNulty, "Children's Books for Christmas," *New Yorker*, December 5, 1983.

140. Judy Blume, "On Becoming a Reader," *Hearst Communications*, 1998. http://homearts.com.

141. Quoted in John Neary, "Interview with Judy Blume," *People*, October 16, 1978.

142. Judy Blume, "Judy Blume Talks About Writing," http://www.judyblume.com.

143. Quoted in *Teen Voices*, "Judy Blume Forever," http://www.bostonwomen.com/blume.html.

144. Blume, "Judy Blume Talks About Writing."

145. Dorothy Broderick, "Review of *Are You There God? It's Me, Margaret*," *New York Times Book Review*, November 8, 1970.

146. Lavinia Russ, "Review of *Are You There God? It's Me, Margaret*," *Publisher's Weekly*, January 11, 1971.

147. R. A. Siegal, "Are You There God? It's Me, Me, Me!" *The Lion and the Unicorn*, Fall 1978.

148. Quoted in Ray Suarez, "Talk of the Nation: Judy Blume." Washington, DC: National Public Radio, October 21, 1998.

149. Blume, "Judy Blume Talks About Writing."

150. Oppenheimer, "Why Judy Blume Endures."

151. Barbara Rollock, "The World of Children's Literature—Radio Interview with Judy Blume." New York: WNYC, November 31, 1977.

152. Quoted in Michelle Green, "After Two Divorces, Judy Blume Blossoms as an Unmarried Woman," *People Weekly,* March 19, 1984.

153. Quoted in Isabel Vincent, "A Heroine for Children," *Globe and Mail,* November 17, 1990.

154. Quoted in Suarez, "Talk of the Nation: Judy Blume."

155. Don Gallo, "What Teachers Should Know About YA Lit for 2004," *English Journal,* November 1984.

FOR FURTHER READING

Anne Arnott, *The Secret Country of C. S. Lewis.* Grand Rapids, MI: William B. Eerdmans, 1975. The life of Lewis told in story form for middle school and young adult readers.

Julie Berg, *E. B. White: A Tribute to the Young at Heart.* Edina, MN: Abdo & Daughters, 1994. A short, simple biography for young readers.

Julie Berg, *Maurice Sendak.* Edina, MN: Abdo & Daughters, 1993. A short book for young readers outlining the major points of Sendak's career.

Judy Blume, *Letters to Judy: What Your Kids Wish They Could Tell You.* New York: G. P. Putnam's Sons, 1986. Copies of letters children sent to Blume and her advice back to them.

David R. Collins, *To the Point: A Story About E. B. White.* Minneapolis: CarolRhoda Books, 1989. With a light touch, the author relays the important points in White's life.

Roald Dahl, *Boy.* New York: Farrar, Straus, Giroux, 1984. An easy-to-read, enjoyable autobiography of Dahl's childhood.

Roald Dahl, *Going Solo.* New York: Farrar, Straus, Giroux, 1986. Dahl goes into detail about the years of his life he spent in Africa and in World War II.

Roald Dahl, *The Wonderful Story of Henry Sugar and Six More.* New York: Knopf, 1977. Six tales of fantasy and a short autobiography on writing.

Thomas Fensch, ed., *Of Sneetches and Whos and the Good Dr. Seuss: Essays on the Writings and Life of Theodor Geisel.* Jefferson, NC: McFarland, 1997. An invaluable collection of twenty-six newspaper and magazine articles, academic essays, and interviews written about Geisel and the importance of his work; written at different stages of his life and career, it gives fascinating insight of his journey.

Beverly Gherman, *E. B. White: Some Writer!* New York: Atheneum, 1992. A straightforward look into White's life and influences.

Douglas Gilbert and Clyde S. Kilby, *C. S. Lewis: Images of His World.* Grand Rapids, MI: Eerdmans, 1973. Photographs of where Lewis lived and worked accompanied by text.

In Search of Dr. Seuss (videorecording). Atlanta: Turner Home Entertainment, 1994. A fun-filled, celebrity-filled live-action/animated exploration of the life and works of Dr. Seuss.

Selma G. Lanes, *The Art of Maurice Sendak*. New York: Harry N. Abrams, 1980. A huge and beautifully rendered book filled with artwork exploring Sendak's books.

Betsy Lee, *Judy Blume's Story*. Minneapolis: Dillon Press, 1981. An easy-to-read biography of Blume's life up to 1981.

C. S. Lewis, *Letters to Children*. Ed. Lyle W. Dorsett and Marjorie Lamp Mead. New York: Macmillan, 1985. Lewis kept copies of his correspondence, and his replies to the children who wrote him letters are reprinted here.

C. S. Lewis, *Surprised by Joy: The Shape of My Early Life*. London: Geoffrey Bles, 1955. Lewis's autobiography about his early years and his conversion to Christianity.

A. A. Milne, *Autobiography*. New York: Dutton, 1939. Milne explores his own childhood and speaks briefly of the effect the Pooh books had on his life.

Maurice Sendak, *Caldecott & Co.: Notes on Books & Pictures*. New York: Farrar, Straus, Giroux, 1988. An indispensable book put together by Sendak himself; a collection of his speeches and essays on the art of writing and illustrating for children.

Brian Sibley, *The Land of Narnia: Brian Sibley Explores the World of C. S. Lewis*. New York: Harper and Row, 1989. A playful "coffeetable" guidebook into Narnia mingled with facts about Lewis's life; includes full-color illustrations by the original illustrator, Pauline Baynes.

Ann Thwaite, *The Brilliant Career of Winnie-the-Pooh*. New York: Dutton's Children's Books, 1994. Traces the life of Milne and Pooh with the use of photographs, newspaper articles, and personal letters; a very enjoyable journey.

Janice Tingum, *E. B. White: The Elements of a Writer*. Minneapolis: Lerner, 1995. An easy-to-read and thorough recounting of White's life; includes many interesting photographs.

Maryann N. Weidt, *Oh, the Places He Went: A Story About Dr. Seuss*. Minneapolis: CarolRhoda Books, 1994. The highlights of Dr. Seuss's career; for young readers.

Maryann N. Weidt, *Presenting Judy Blume*. Boston: Twayne, 1990. A thorough examination of Blume's life focusing on her work.

WORKS CONSULTED

Books

John Cech, *Angels and Wild Things: The Archetypal Poetics of Maurice Sendak*. University Park: Pennsylvania State University Press, 1995. A scholarly approach to dissecting the layers of Sendak's work.

James T. Como, ed., *C. S. Lewis at the Breakfast Table and Other Reminiscences*. New York: Macmillan, 1979. A collection of heartfelt memories of Lewis by the people in his life who knew and loved him best.

Paula T. Connolly, *Winnie-the-Pooh and The House at Pooh Corner: Recovering Arcadia*. New York: Twayne, 1995. A scholarly approach to the meanings behind the Pooh stories.

Marcus Crouch, *Treasure Seekers and Borrowers: Children's Books in Britain*. London: Library Association, 1962. A look at important fantasy children's books by British writers.

Scott Elledge, *E. B. White: A Biography*. New York: W. W. Norton, 1984. A comprehensive, in-depth authorized biography published a year before White's death.

Roger L. Green and Walter Hooper, *C. S. Lewis: A Biography*. London: Collins, 1974. Authorized by Lewis to collaborate on this comprehensive biography, Green was one of Lewis's closest friends, and Hooper was perhaps Lewis's biggest fan.

Dorothy Lobrano Guth, ed. and compiler, *Letters of E. B. White*. New York: Harper, 1976. A wonderful collection and a great way to get to know White, a constant letter writer, better.

Myra Kibler, *Dictionary of Literary Biography*. Vol. 61, *American Writers for Children Since 1960*. Detroit, MI: Gale, 1987. Dictionary of short biographies on popular authors.

E. L. Konigsburg, *TalkTalk: A Children's Book Author Speaks to Grown-Ups*. New York: Atheneum, 1995. The award-winning author talks about her life and her writing.

C. S. Lewis, *On Stories and Other Essays on Literature*. Ed. Walter Hooper. New York: Harcourt Brace Jovanovich, 1982. Twenty essays and lectures by Lewis; compiled after his death and printed in England under the title *Of These and Other Worlds*.

W. H. Lewis, *Letters of C. S. Lewis*. New York: Harcourt, Brace & World, 1966. A collection of decades of correspondence compiled by Lewis's brother, Warnie; an excellent way to get to know the man.

Alison Lurie, *Don't Tell the Grown-Ups: Subversive Children's Literature.* Boston: Little, Brown, 1990. A study by the Pulitzer prize–winning author of how the best-loved children's books tend to challenge rather than uphold the values of adults.

Ruth K. MacDonald, *Dr. Seuss.* Boston: Twayne, 1988. An in-depth, critical interpretation of the works, intentions, legacy, and life of Dr. Seuss.

A. A. Milne, *By Way of Introduction.* London: Methuen, 1929. Milne talks about his motivation for writing the Pooh books.

A. A. Milne, *The House at Pooh Corner.* New York: Dutton, 1928. The sequel to *Winnie-the-Pooh.*

Christopher Milne, *The Enchanted Places.* New York: Dutton, 1975. A. A. Milne's son talks about his own life and experiences.

Judith and Neil Morgan, *Dr. Seuss and Mr. Geisel: A Biography.* New York: Random House, 1995. A fascinating in-depth look into the life of Dr. Seuss, written by two journalists who knew him for nearly thirty years.

Peter Neumeyer, *Annotated Charlotte's Web.* New York: HarperCollins, 1994. *Charlotte's Web* with a new introduction discussing its importance in history.

Isabel Russell, *Katharine and E. B. White: An Affectionate Memoir.* New York: W. W. Norton, 1988. Insights into the home life of the Whites, written by their personal secretary.

Anita Silvey, ed., *Children's Books and Their Creators.* Boston: Houghton Mifflin, 1995. A large and thorough examination of hundreds of children's authors; includes many interviews.

Amy Sonheim, *Maurice Sendak.* New York: Twayne, 1991. An approachable critical look at Sendak's life and career.

Ann Thwaite, *A. A. Milne: The Man Behind Winnie-the-Pooh.* New York: Random House, 1990. A very detailed biography, drawing on a large number of personal sources.

John Rowe Townsend, *Twentieth Century Children's Literature.* Ed. Tracy Chevalier. Chicago: St. James Press, 1989. A compendium of children's literature.

Jeremy Treglown, *Roald Dahl: A Biography.* New York: Farrar, Straus, Giroux, 1994. A very thorough and, at times, critical examination of Dahl's life.

Mark I. West, *Roald Dahl.* New York: Twayne, 1992. An examination of Dahl's works and a short look at his life.

Mark I. West, *Trust Your Children: Voices Against Censorship in Children's Literature.* New York: Neal-Schuman, 1988. Authors speak out on the harm that censoring books does to children.

E. B. White, *Essays of E. B. White.* New York: Harper and Row, 1977. A collection of White's finest essays from various sources.

E. B. White, *One Man's Meat: A New and Enlarged Edition.* New York: Harper & Brothers, 1944. A collection of articles from *Harper's* magazine.

E. B. White, *The Points of My Compass: Essays.* New York: Harper, 1962. White talks about his early years.

E. B. White, *Second Tree from the Corner.* New York: Harper, 1954.

A. N. Wilson, *C. S. Lewis: A Biography.* New York: W. W. Norton, 1990. A thorough examination of Lewis's life.

Jackie Wullschlager, *Inventing Wonderland.* New York: Free Press, 1995. A study of Victorian childhood as seen through the eyes of the authors who made it famous.

Periodicals

Roger Angell, "E. B. White," *New Yorker,* October 14, 1985.

Dorothy Broderick, "Review of *Are You There God? It's Me, Margaret,*" *New York Times Book Review,* November 8, 1970.

Peter Bunzel, "The Wacky World of Dr. Seuss Delights the Child—and Adult—Readers of His Books," *Life,* April 6, 1959.

Bennett Cerf, *Saturday Review,* Jan. 3, 1953.

Jay Copp, "A Touch of Narnia in Illinois," *Christian Science Monitor,* March 23, 1999.

Charlotte Cory, "Life Story: The Woman Who Drew Narnia," *Daily Telegraph,* September 19, 1998.

Naomi Decter, "Judy Blume's Children," *Commentary,* March 1980.

Don Freeman, "Dr. Seuss at 72—Going Like 60," *Saturday Evening Post,* March 1977.

Don Gallo, "What Teachers Should Know About YA Lit for 2004," *English Journal,* November 1984.

Arthur Gordon, "The Wonderful Wizard of Soledad Hill," *Women's Day,* September 1965.

Michelle Green, "After Two Divorces, Judy Blume Blossoms as an Unmarried Woman," *People Weekly,* March 19, 1984.

Gerald Haigh, "For Non Squiffletrotters Only," *Times Educational Supplement,* November 19, 1982.

Karen Hershenson, "Kids Love Author's Black Humor, but Many Adults Have Their Doubts," *Contra Costa Times,* April 24, 1996.

ICA Video, "Writing for Children." Northbrook, IL: Roland Collection, 1992.

E. J. Kahn Jr., "Children's Friend," *New Yorker,* December 17, 1960.

Alfred A. Knopf, *Letter from July 5, 1960.* Archives of Alfred A. Knopf, Inc., Harry Ransom Humanities Research Center at the University of Texas at Austin.

Adam Langer, "Maurice Sendak: Dancing with Wolves," *Book Magazine,* May/June 1999.

Edward Connery Lathem, ed., "The Beginnings of Dr. Seuss: A Conversation with Theodor S. Geisel," *Dartmouth Alumni Magazine,* April 1976.

Life, "The World of Pooh Lives On," February 1956.

Faith McNulty, "Children's Books for Christmas," *New Yorker,* December 5, 1983.

Faith McNulty, "Children's Books for Christmas," *New Yorker,* November 25, 1991.

John Neary, "Interview with Judy Blume," *People,* October 16, 1978.

New York Times, "The Librarian Said It Was Bad for Children," March 6, 1966.

Mark Oppenheimer, "Why Judy Blume Endures," *New York Times Book Review,* November 16, 1997.

Willa Petschek, "Roald Dahl at Home," *New York Times Book Review,* December 25, 1977.

Phoebe Pettingell, "Writers and Writing: C. S. Lewis' Romantic Egoism," *New Leader,* March 19, 1990.

Publisher's Weekly, "Dr. Seuss Remembered," October 25, 1991.

Barbara Rollock, "The World of Children's Literature—Radio Interview with Judy Blume." New York: WNYC, November 31, 1977.

Lavinia Russ, "Review of *Are You There God? It's Me, Margaret,*" *Publisher's Weekly,* January 11, 1971.

Glenn Edward Sadler, "Maurice Sendak and Dr. Seuss: A Conversation," *Horn Book Magazine,* September/October 1989.

Martha Shirk, "Gloomy Relatives Inspired Wild Things," *St. Louis Post-Dispatch,* December 4, 1989.

R. A. Siegal, "Are You There God? It's Me, Me, Me!" *The Lion and the Unicorn,* Fall 1978.

Anita Silvey, "The Problem with Trends," *Horn Book Magazine,* September/October 1995.

Sybil Steinberg, "PW Interviews: Judy Blume," *Publisher's Weekly,* April 17, 1978.

James Stewart-Gordon, "Dr. Seuss: Fanciful State of Childhood," *Reader's Digest,* April 1972.

Ray Suarez, "Talk of the Nation: Judy Blume." Washington, DC: National Public Radio, October 21, 1998.

Isabel Vincent, "A Heroine for Children," *Globe and Mail,* November 17, 1990.

E. B. White, "A Strategem for Retirement," *Holiday*, March 1956.

E. B. White, "On Writing for Children," *Paris Review 48*, Fall 1969.

Internet Sources

John Banbury, "The Art of Maurice Sendak," November, 1997. http://libserver.lib.flinders.edu.au/resources/collection/special/exhib/sendak.htm.

Judy Blume, "Judy Blume Talks About Writing," http://www.judyblume.com.

Judy Blume, "On Becoming a Reader," Hearst Communications, 1998. http://homearts.com

Marion Long, "Maurice Sendak: A Western Canon," http://homearts.com/depts/relat/sendakfl.htm.

Teen Voices, "Judy Blume Forever," http:www.bostonwomen.com/blume.html.

INDEX

PICTURE CREDITS

ABOUT THE AUTHOR

Wendy Mass holds a B.A. in English from Tufts University and an M.A. in Creative Writing from California State University, Long Beach. She is the cofounder and editor of a national literary journal for teenagers called *Writes of Passage* and is the author of fiction and nonfiction books and articles for young adults. She has worked as a book editor for Longmeadow Press and Reader's Digest Young Families.